WORLD RELIGIONS IN BRIEF

Gary E. Antion and Douglas Ruml

iUniverse, Inc.
Bloomington

World Religions in Brief

iUniverse books may be ordered through booksellers or by contacting:

iUniverse
1663 Liberty Drive
Bloomington, IN 47403
www.iuniverse.com
1-800-Authors (1-800-288-4677)

ISBN: 978-1-4502-6173-9 (pbk)
ISBN: 978-1-4502-6174-6 (ebk)

Printed in the United States of America

iUniverse rev. date: 1/6/11

CONTENTS

Introduction vii

Section I — World Religions

Tribal Religions.. 3
Hinduism 6
Jainism... 13
Buddhism 17
Sikhism... 23
Taoism.. 27
Confucianism.. 33
Shintoism 38
Zoroastrianism 41
Judaism 45
Christianity.. 53
Islam 59

Section II — Christian Denominations

Roman Catholicism... 67
Orthodox Christians 73
Anglicans / Episcopalians.. 78
Lutherans.. 82
Presbyterians 86
Methodists... 90
Baptists 94
Anabaptists: Mennonites, Amish And The Brethren........................ 97
Society Of Friends (Quakers)... 101
Seventh Day Adventists 104
Church Of Jesus Christ Of The Latter Day Saints............................ 108
Church Of Christ Scientist Christian Science................................ 113
Salvation Army 116
Jehovah's Witnesses... 119
Pentecostals / Charismatics 123

Appendices

1. *Magic, Religion and Man*.. 129
2. *Chinese Folk Religion* 136
3. *Caste System in Hinduism* 139
4. *Nirvana in Buddhism* 141
5. *A Day of Rest*... 143
6. *Point of Origin and Philosophy of World Religions*.................... 153
7. *The Golden Rule in Various Traditions* 154
8. *Similarities Among the World's Religions*............................. 156
9. *Apostles' Creed*... 158
10. *Selections from:*... 159
11. *Selected Illustrations* 161
12. *World Religions Glossary*.. 182
13. *Christian Denominations Glossary*..................................... 186

Bibliography 189

INTRODUCTION

"For although religion does not explain everything about a people's behavior, as the mother of morals and definer of justice it has ever been a chief arbiter of man's conduct." (Anon., *The Path of Buddhism*, 20).

Our goal in writing this book is to make the religious beliefs of the majority of humanity understandable to those who do not come from the same religious background. They are each greatly summarized. Thus, the point needs to be made that each section consists of what could be called "orthodox generalizations", and that the personal beliefs of individuals or of sects within the various religious traditions will be quite different in some areas covered.

In the main section of this book, we have striven to use material from each religion about itself (such as denominational pamphlets, correspondence courses, conversations with believers and interviews with clergy), with our own additional commentary supplied only in order to make ideas foreign to the North American mind more easily grasped. If we have confused, or rendered anything inaccurate it is our own misunderstanding of the material that we consulted, and the fault is ours alone. In addition, several appendices have been added in order to examine some areas of special interest (at least for us) in greater depth. These appendices are written from our own perspectives.

After spending so much time overseas (Douglas) and with so many international university students (Gary), we became intrigued by how much better we could understand and be accepted by people of other cultures if we got to know a little about their religions (or the religion that influenced the culture that they were raised in). Rather than just knowing geography and perhaps a bit of political news (as you would tend to get from the media or a modern/western program, article or book about a place), knowing religion helps in being able to relate to others culturally, even if they are not practicing a religion.

It seems that religions and cultures are very tightly interrelated. So tightly, in fact, that having knowledge of the 3 general categories of religions which came out of the 3 areas of the world (China, India, Near East) gives a person a real advantage in better understanding both people and cultures. Although we are largely dealing with generalizations, we have sought to find a tentative starting point in discussing things that a novice might otherwise lack. The first half of this book is devoted to religions beyond Christianity. As the world increasingly becomes a smaller place, a basic understanding of the different religions of others that one increasingly meets at work and socially will become more important.

We have spent much of the book describing the many branches of Christianity. This was not only because it happens to be the authors' religious background, but also because it gives a perspective of how much variation exists in the largest religion in the world today. The Orthodoxy of the Middle Ages can no longer be seen in the lives of individual Christians, let alone their hundreds and hundreds of church organizations. People used to think that religions were monolithic, but they turn out to be much more heterodox than was originally assumed.

It is our prayer that this book will prove helpful and useful to the reader in better understanding all the varied beliefs of humanity and that it may be a tool for the user to also come to better understand other people of whatever religious background.

Finally, we'd like to acknowledge Amanda Stiver for her relentless job of editing our often messy manuscript, and Michelle de Campos for the beautiful cover she designed for this book.

Gary Antion, MA   Douglas Ruml, CFM, MA

SECTION I

—

WORLD RELIGIONS

TRIBAL RELIGIONS

(c. 244 million adherents)

FOUNDER:

No particular one individual, though individuals from various nationalities have given their particular tribal religion its uniqueness and direction. These may have included priests, shamans, witch doctors or philosophers.

GOD(s):

Usually various gods or deities of tribe, village, nature or ancestors. Followers often look beyond the gods to a single creator God who is above all gods. The spirits or deities receive their strength from the supreme God.

SCRIPTURES:

Various traditions and tribal legends and rituals that were handed down mainly by oral history. Some regulations may be altered as generations change and practices become obsolete.

HISTORY:

There is no single history that covers the various tribal religions. Many seem to have developed according to happenings in nature and fear of certain events (lightning, thunder, earthquakes for example) that were not understood. Normal happenings in life – birth, adulthood, marriage, and death – gave reason for rejoicing or sorrowing. This caused the followers to look to a higher power.

BELIEFS AND CHARACTERISTICS:

Some Common Features:

1. Animism: Nature and the world around is alive with spirits and mystical forces (personal or impersonal), thus <u>objects and natural phenomena</u> are worshipped and venerated.

2. Magic: Attempting to force nature to one's will. *Sympathetic Magic* attempts to coerce nature to behave in a certain manner by performing that act oneself on a smaller scale (example: voodoo dolls).

3. Divination: Seeing into the future, usually through the use of a Shaman.

4. Taboo: Certain actions and objects must be avoided so as not to anger the spirit world.

5. Totems: Some primitive religions express the kinship they feel with nature, for example, identifying themselves with particular animals.

6. Sacrifice: One of the most common practices of all religions. It is variously considered in terms of feeding the spirits, giving a gift to the spirits, or establishing a bond between men and the spirits.

7. Rites of Passage: Certain rituals are carried out at key points in the life of a person.

8. Fetish – an object that controls nature in a magical fashion (example: lucky rabbits' feet).

9. Worship of Ancestors: Believing that the soul lives on after the death of the body, led to efforts to avert the evil the dead might do. Positively, ancestors are also worshipped to please the dead so they will benefit the living.

- Evil is caused by human mistakes, chance and malicious sorcery.

- Goal is to fulfill one's particular destiny now (a tribal position, attaining old age, dying of natural causes, bearing children). Salvation, or the future, is not much considered.

- For spiritual help tribal members go to the diviners or seek help from ancestor spirits.

- Worship consists of family rites, personal prayers, use of religious objects, and offerings made to a deity.

- Circumcision is practiced in some tribes (such as in New Guinea).

- Shamans or holy men help reveal the will of God to the laity.

- With some tribes, possession by a spirit of the deity is desirable.

HUMANITY:

Belief in the immortal soul concept. Some believe a person has two souls. One goes off to where the dead go (there is no heaven -hell concept) after hovering around the cemetery. The other stays around the family shrine in the home. When a "special" child is born with unique features, it is thought that the ancestor has been reincarnated. Most of man's purpose is concerned with the present life with little thought of the afterlife. When dead, it is believed that the spirit or soul that lives on is more powerful than when the person was alive.

LOCATION:

These tribal religions are today only found in the more underdeveloped areas of the world: pockets in Africa, the Americas, Australia, Asia and the isles of the Pacific.

HINDUISM

(c. 820 million adherents)

FOUNDER:

Hinduism (or Vedanta ["The religion of the Vedas"], as has been suggested) is a religion without a Founder; unlike Christianity, Islam, Buddhism, or even Judaism. Further, there is no precise date of when the religious system (or set of interrelated religious beliefs) began, only that they grew up somewhat organically between 1500 BC and 400 BC.

GOD(s):

Brahman: "World Soul" is a three-in-one god or Trimurti.

1. Brahma: Creator who is largely ignored in worship.
2. Vishnu: Preserver who is actively worshipped (particularly as Krishna).
3. Shiva: Destroyer who is both worshipped and feared.

Millions of lesser gods or spirits are also revered.

SCRIPTURES:

One of the primary beliefs held in common by Hindus is the validity of their holy scriptures, the *Vedas*, as the inspired word of God. They are largely hymns and rituals of priests; the *Rig Veda* is the oldest and most important of these. The *Upanishads* are commentaries on the *Vedas*. Another work, the *Bhagavad-Gita* ("The Lord's Song") is an epic poem which is the most influential document in the religious history of India.

HISTORY:

The development of Hinduism began when the Aryans, led by rajahs or chieftains, invaded India from Persia sometime around 1700-1500 BC. They were Indo-Europeans and brought the worship of multiple gods with them. Their beliefs became mixed with the native Indian traditions to form what we now know as Hinduism. The caste structure, for instance, can be traced back to this time and the desire to have a stable social foundation after the invaders had consolidated power.

From 500 BC to 500 AD internal difficulties, both political and economic, caused the religion to undergo further modification (from what is termed "Classical" to "Modern" Hinduism). These changes brought the religion closer in line with the character and beliefs of the Indian people at that time.

Later, the Hindus had to endure 750 years of subjugation by Muslims (999 to 1757 AD). Two great areas of the Indian subcontinent today are Islamic (Pakistan and Bangladesh) as a result of this invasion. In India itself about 15% of the population is Muslim.

More recently, Christianity did not successfully leave its mark on India, when the Europeans (mainly the British) dominated India from 1757 to 1947. The British did end the practice of Suttee (ritual killing of wives upon the death of their husbands) and the depredations of the Thugs (violent devotees of Shiva the Destroyer's wife Bhavani). The British influence also introduced democracy and an open questioning on the caste system (particularly as regards the untouchables). One of the most famous modern Hindus was Mahatma Gandhi (1869-1948) who, through his pacifism, fasting and application of Hindu ethical principles, led the Indians to independence. Hinduism remains the dominant religion of India and of Indian communities around the world.

BELIEFS AND CHARACTERISTICS:

Hinduism can seem very chaotic and is inclusive, absorbing teachings and even deities from other religions (for instance, Jesus Christ is accepted as a god by Hinduism).

7

- Karma – good from good, evil from evil, the law of cause and effect. It is the force that binds the soul to an endless cycle of death and rebirth (Reincarnation) unless it is broken. Another way of thinking about Karma is to understand that it is a way of explaining that when bad things happen to you in this life, it is because of deeds you did in a past life (and vice versa).

- Transmigration of Souls – The universe is alive with a great Transmigration of Souls that is constantly going on. A person is really an immortal soul (Atman) which is separated from the soul of the universe (Brahman), and doomed to endless reincarnation unless the cycle is broken. The reincarnated soul moves from caste to caste in various lives. Many Hindu believe that souls are destined to inhabit the bodies of both humans and beasts until released.

- Moksha – the ultimate goal in life: to learn to deny the world and thus achieve release and thus to become at one with the universal spirit.

- Personal Salvation can be obtained in a number of ways:

  1. Jnana – Knowledge (asceticism).
  2. Karma – Deeds (obedience to caste rules).
  3. Bhakti – Devotion (worship of the gods).
  4. Raja – Meditation.

- The Four Goals of human life are:

  1. Dharma: specified duties of one's caste
  2. Artha: worldly concern – how to get along with the world legitimately
  3. Kama: pursuit of love and pleasure
  4. Moksha: the ultimate goal of release and the expansion of consciousness in going back to Brahman.

- No Founder and No Fixed Creed.

- Hindu Religious Practice is very personal.

- Two Common Beliefs of All Hindus:

1. Validity of the Vedas – as the inspired word of the World Soul.
2. Caste system – all people are born into one of four levels or castes:

    1. Brahmin – holy men
    2. Kshatriya – rulers and warriors
    3. Vaishyas – merchants and craftsmen
    4. Sudras – commoners

Each caste has its own specialized duties (Dharma).
[Please see Appendix 3 for more information on the Caste system]

- Philosophical Hinduism teaches that there is only Brahman, the "World Soul", who/which is God. The way it is perceived by people (which is to say in a way comprehendible to the limited beings that we are) is sometimes as a three-in-one god or Trimurti.

- Both Vishnu and Shiva have numerous aspects and avatars, as do their respective wives. Vishnu, for example, had many avatars or appearances: fish, tortoise, dwarf, Rama, Krishna, Buddha. His last appearance is yet to come. In it, Kalkin, a warrior, will appear on a white steed with a flaming sword and will judge the evil ones, reward the righteous and set up an ideal world.

- Beyond (or perhaps below) the three primary gods there are also millions of lesser gods and spirits which are also reverenced. Most typical Hindu relate to their gods as individuals, rather than in reference to "ultimate reality" (as in Philosophical Hinduism).

- Ideal life cycle of man in Hinduism (from the Code of Manu) as a man grows older:

    1. Student
    2. Householder
    3. Hermit
    4. Wandering beggar

- The Cow is sacred because it exemplifies non-aggression and non-materialism.

HUMANITY:

Has an immortal soul, separated from the soul of the universe, doomed to endless reincarnation unless the cycle is broken.

- There is seemingly no purpose to this life except to seek to be released from the endless cycle of death and rebirth and to be united with the spirit of the universe through works.

- Salvation from the cycle of death and rebirth is through works. Works can be rituals, good deeds, meditation, or devotion to God.

- Humans are souls destined to inhabit the bodies of men and beasts until finally released.

LOCATION:

India, Bali, Indian communities throughout the world.

SAYINGS OF HINDUISM

"In this world a two-fold basis (of religion) has been declared by Me of old, blameless one:
By the discipline of knowledge of the followers of reason-method, And by the discipline of action of the followers of discipline-method"

"For desired enjoyments to you the gods
Will give, prospered by worship;
Without giving to them, their gifts
Whoso enjoys, is nothing but a thief."

"Good men who eat the remnants of (food offered in) worship
Are freed from all sins;
But those wicked men eat evil
Who cook for their own selfish sakes."

"All actions of the senses And actions of breath, others of the fire of the discipline of control of self Offer up, when it has been kindled by knowledge."

"Learn to know this by obeisance (to those who can teach it), By questioning (them), by serving (them); They will teach thee knowledge, Those who have knowledge, who see the truth."

"The man of faith gets knowledge, Intent solely upon it, restraining his senses. Having got knowledge, to supreme peace In no long time he goes."

"Fearlessness, purification of essence,
Steadfastness in the discipline of knowledge,
Generosity, control, and religious worship,
Study of the Holy Word, austerities, uprightness,
Harmlessness, truth, no anger,
Abandonment, serenity, no backbiting,
Compassion towards creatures, no greedy desire,
Gentleness, modesty, no fickleness,"

"There are two creations of beings in this world, The divine and the demoniac."

"Without truth, without religious basis, they Say is the world, without a God, Not originating in regular mutual causation; In short, motivated by desire alone."

"Egotism, force, pride,
Desire, and wrath they have taken to,
Me in their own and others' bodies
Hating, these envious men.
These cruel and hateful
Base men, in the ceaseless round of existences,
These wicked ones, I constantly hurl
Into demoniac wombs alone."

"Men of goodness worship the gods, Men of passion sprites and ogres, To ghosts and the hordes of goblins others, The folk of darkness, pay worship."

11

"Actions of worship, gift, and austerity
Must not be abandoned, but rather performed;
Worship, gift, and austerity
Are purifiers of the wise."

(The quotations above were taken from *Bhagavad-Gita*)

"Find the reward of doing right, in right."

"That man alone is wise who remains master of himself."

"Do your allotted task! Work excels idleness."

"To die performing duty is no ill."

"Knowing truth, your heart will ache no more with error."

"Whoever offers Me in faith and love a leaf, a flower, a fruit, or water poured forth, that offering made lovingly, with pious will, I accept."

"Those who worship me with love, I love; they are in me, and I in them."

"The fruit of lust is pain and toil."

"The fruit of ignorance is deeper darkness."

"Religion shown in act of proud display is rash and vain."

(The quotations above were taken from *What the Great Religions Believe* by Joseph Gaer.)

JAINISM

(c. 5.5 million adherents)

FOUNDER:

Nataputta Vardhamana, known as Mahavira ("Great Hero"). He lived from 599 to 527 B.C.

GOD(S):

The 24 Tirthaṇkaras ("Crossing Builders") – ideal men who linked this life with Nirvana.

SCRIPTURES:

Agamas ("precepts") or *Siddhantas* ("treatises"). The various Jain sects differ as to which are the authoritative sermons of Mahavira.

HISTORY:

23 figures preceded Mahavira in the founding of Jainism, according to legend, building a bridge between this life and Nirvana.

Mahavira was born into the Kshatriya Caste in Northern India – the second son of a minor ruler. A wealthy young man, he married and had a daughter, but was unhappy and sought a religious answer through extreme asceticism and "Ahimsa" (non-injury to any living thing). He became known as a "Jain" (conqueror) because he achieved release from endless cycle of birth and death after 12 years of asceticism. Living another 30 years he died at age 72.

By 80 A.D. Jainism was divided into two sects – the liberal Svetambara ("White Clad") whose monks wear clothes, and the orthodox Digambara ("Sky Clad") whose monks wander around nearly nude, and who believe women cannot obtain salvation. A third sect arose in 1473, the Sthanakavasi, who oppose all idols and temples.

Because of Ahimsa and their honesty the Jains tend to do well in business. There are fewer than 2 million "pure" Jains today.

BELIEFS AND CHARACTERISTICS:

- The soul is trapped in matter and can be released through severe asceticism.

- The individual must work out salvation – thus the gods are unimportant.

- Vows: All Jains try to keep the first three vows; monks try to keep all five:

  1. Non-injury of life (Ahimsa). They eat vegetables (preferably left over from someone else's meal), strain water lest they drink any creatures in the water, sweep the ground before them lest they step on and crush any bugs, and have been known to found hospitals for sick rats.
  2. Always speak the truth (which they consider to be relative).
  3. Don't take anything not given to them.
  4. Renounce sexual pleasures.
  5. Renounce all attachments.

HUMANITY:

A soul trapped in a body or even in the stones, air, dust, etc., and which can be released through asceticism.

Since Jains work out their own salvation through ascetic practices, the 24 Tirthankaras, though venerated, are of little importance in their spiritual development.

LOCATION:

India, particularly around Bombay.

SAYINGS OF JAINISM

"All things are eternal by their very nature."

"The world is boundless and eternal; it exists for eternity and shall not perish."

"Men suffer individually for the deeds they themselves have done." "Knowing the truth, one should live up to it."

"They who spend much time with women cease to practice meditation."

"Reckless men who cut down sprouts out of regard for their own pleasure, destroy many living creatures."

"A wise man should abstain from: fame, glory, and renown; honors, respectful treatment, and all pleasures of this world."

"He who is carried away by passion will not get very far."

"He who knows the truth is kind to his fellow creatures."

"Who recognizes that he sins and does not cease from sinning is called a foolish man."

(The quotations above were taken from *What the Great Religions Believe* by Joseph Gaer.)

"By one's actions one becomes a Brahmana, or a Kshatriya, or a Vaishya, or a Sudra."

"Right belief is conviction in one' s own self."

"Charity without faith can never be the means of salvation."

"Difficult to conquer is oneself. But when that is conquered everything is conquered."

"A man should wonder about treating all creatures as he himself would be treated."

"Man! Thou art thine own friend. Why wishest thou for a friend beyond thyself."

"That which is given once is received back a thousand times."

"One must worship God, serve the Guru, study the scriptures, control the senses, perform austerities, and give alms."

"Harmlessness is the only religion."

"Do not kill living beings in any of three ways, by mind, word or deed."
"The wise should know the Law."

"Love conquers all."

"All men in due time must suffer the fruit of their works."

(The quotations above were taken from *The Eleven Religions and Their Proverbial Lore* by Selwyn G. Champion.)

BUDDHISM

(c. 369 million adherents)

FOUNDER:

Siddhartha Gautama (The Buddha or "Enlightened One") *(563-483 B.C.)*

GOD(S):

In Theravada Buddhism gods are of little importance; the Buddha himself is reverenced in the temples.

In Mahayana Buddhism it is believed that the Buddha was a compassionate divine being. Thus Mahayana Buddhism absorbs other gods by saying they are incarnations of the Buddha.

SCRIPTURES:

In Theravada Buddhism: the *Triptaka* is used, a collection of legends and stories about the Buddha and his teachings.

In Mahayana Buddhism: *Lotus Sutra*, a handbook is used.

HISTORY:

Siddhartha Gautama lived in northern India during the sixth century B.C. As a son of a Rajah, he was brought up as a prince. Siddhartha learned the five arts: riding, fencing, painting, composing love lyrics and dancing. In his royal upbringing, Siddhartha was shielded from the world and human misery. He was raised a Hindu.

One day on a trip outside his sheltered surroundings, he saw four sights that made a deep impression upon him. He saw an old-aged man, a diseased man, a dead person, and a monk. He was greatly distressed. He began to wonder about life and its meaning. These feelings burned so deeply that around the age of 30 he decided to leave his home and family and wandered for six years searching for meaning and purpose.

First Siddhartha tried learning more from the gurus or teachers. Then he turned to asceticism in an effort to understand life. He lived for days at a time with only one bean for his daily meal. He became so emaciated that he said that when he tried to touch his stomach, he actually felt his spine! He almost died of malnutrition before some of his friends revived him with food and water. He then decided that life should not be lived to extremes. He meditated under a fig tree (or bo tree) to receive enlightenment as to the meaning of life. At the conclusion of his meditation, he felt he had "seen the light." He became the Buddha ("The Enlightened One").

He traveled to the city of Benares and gave his first sermon at the Deer Park there. Because of his preaching of a "Middle Way" of life (i.e. balanced, not extreme), the Four Noble Truths, and his denial of the strict caste system, he had wide appeal and gathered followers. His disciples exported their faith to Eastern Asia where Buddhism today flourishes more than in the Buddha's native India. The Buddha never intended to set himself up as an object of worship, but said a person honors him by practicing his teachings in the best manner. Buddha died by eating poison mushrooms served accidentally by a friend.

There are many statues of the Buddha in various poses – most showing meditation. The image varies according to the sect and country in which it is located.

BELIEFS AND CHARACTERISTICS:

- Four Noble Truths:

    1. Suffering comes through bodily senses
    2. Suffering comes from desire
    3. Desire can end
    4. Release is accomplished by the "eight-fold path" (the "middle way" of avoiding extremes)

- Eight-Fold Path:

    1. Right Beliefs – clear understanding
    2. Right Resolve – pure-minded, free of desire
    3. Right Speech – not loud or selfish
    4. Right Action - observing the basic five precepts (See Layman's Five Moral Precepts)
    5. Right Vocation
    6. Right Effort – cultivating good deeds and good words
    7. Right Contemplation – state of awareness in body
    8. Right Meditation or Concentration

- Three Jewels:

    1. Buddha – the enlightened one
    2. Dharma – teaching Four Noble Truths
    3. Sangha – order of the monks

- Goal is Nirvana – a "blowing-out" (extinguishing of self and desire); supreme bliss.

- Anyone can find salvation, regardless of caste.

- The soul does not exist – personality doesn't exist forever – no transmigration of souls in same sense as Hinduism (see appendix 4).

- Layman's Five Moral Precepts:

    1. Don't kill
    2. Don't Steal – fair play
    3. Purity and self-control
    4. Don't lie – keep your word
    5. Don't imbibe of intoxicating drinks or drugs

- Monks Also Practice:
    o No solid food after noon
    o Avoid worldly entertainment
    o Renounce ornaments and elaborate clothes
    o Refuse gifts of money
    o Don't sleep on raised bed

Monks may practice 227 rules in all.

- Zen – the belief that enlightenment can be attained through meditation rather than teachings.

- Karma – the law of cause and effect: good from good, evil from evil. Another way of thinking about Karma is to understand that it is a way of explaining that when bad things happen to you in this life (even if you are a good person), it is because of bad deeds you did in a past life. The other side of this would be when a bad person has good things happen to them; it is because of good deeds done in a prior life.

- Two Branches of Buddhism:

  1. Theravada – "Tradition of the elders" is practiced in Sri Lanka, Burma, Thailand, Laos, and Cambodia. Also known as "Hinayana" Buddhism.
  2. Mahayana – "The greater vehicle" is practiced in Nepal, Sikkim, Bhutan, Tibet, China, Mongolia, Vietnam, Korea, and Japan. The type of Mahayana Buddhism practiced in Tibet is known as "Bon" Buddhism.

Comparisons of the Two Major Types:

1. Aspects of Theravada Buddhism:

   o Fewer adherents than Mahayana Buddhism.

     - People must work out their own salvation without reliance on anything other than themselves.
     - The gods are largely ignored; Theravada is a more philosophic approach to religion.

   o Monastic life is for everyone.
   o Conservative

2. Aspects of Mahayana Buddhism:

   o More adherents than Theravada.

o   Worship many divine beings.

- Believe they have the secret truths, and have expanded the Buddha's teachings.
- Salvation can be expedited by obtaining the help of Bodhisattvas ("enlightened beings") – who, similar to saints in medieval Catholic Church theology, were men who made it to heaven with so much merit that they could share it with human kind.

o   Involvement in spirits

o   All men may become Buddhas or god-like beings

o   Liberal

HUMANITY:

The body is like a cloak wrapped around a "soul" which has always existed. The "soul" is like a flow of consciousness that never ceases to exist. This "soul" continues to be purified or defiled depending upon the deeds (Karma) of the person. As one person dies, the state of the soul with its deeds comes alive in a new being until *desire* has been finally conquered through right thoughts and right action. Buddhists maintain that this is not the same as transmigration of souls. What is passed to another is a person's Karma or deeds (see Appendix 4 for a fuller explanation of the differences in this area between Hinduism and Buddhism).

LOCATION:

China, Taiwan, Japan, Korea, Thailand, Burma, Sri Lanka, Singapore, Laos, Cambodia, Vietnam, India

SAYINGS OF BUDDHISM

"All that we are is the result of what we have thought: it is founded on our thoughts and is made up of our thoughts."

"As rain breaks through an ill-thatched roof, so lust breaks through an ill-trained mind."

"Thoughtfulness is the road to immortality (Nirvana); thoughtlessness, the road to death."

"The thoughtful do not die; the thoughtless are as if dead already."

"Fools follow vanity; but the wise man prizes his thoughtfulness as a treasure."

"If a man's faith is unstable and his peace of mind troubled, his knowledge will not be perfect."

"An evil deed, like freshly drawn milk, does not turn sour at once."

"Though a man go out to battle a thousand times against a thousand men, if he conquers himself he is the greater conqueror."

"One's own self is the most difficult to subdue."

"The pure and impure stand and fall by their own deeds; no one can purify another."

"Victory breeds hatred. He who has given up both victory and defeat, he is contented and happy."

"He who has tasted the sweetness of solitude and tranquility becomes free from fear and free from sin."

(The quotations above were taken from *What the Great Religions Believe* by Joseph Gaer.)

SIKHISM

(c. 24 million adherents)

FOUNDER:

Nanak (1469-1538)

GOD(S):

"The True Name" – Creator of the Universe

SCRIPTURES:

The *Granth* – a collection of hymns, many of which were apparently written by Nanak himself.

HISTORY:

A man from the border region of hostile Hindu and Muslim communities, Nanak was influenced by both Hindu and Muslim teachings. He left his wife and moved to Sultanpur, where at age 30 he received a vision from god. His message was to be, "There is no Muslim and there is no Hindu." Nanak and his companion Mardana traveled over India preaching the unity of Islam and Hinduism wearing mixed clothing of both Hindus and Muslims. His followers were called Sikhs ("disciple").

There was a line of ten gurus that led the Sikhs until 1708. The fifth Guru began compiling the official scriptures around 1600 A.D. The Muslims about this time perceived Sikhism as a threat, and when the fifth Guru was tortured to death for not expunging from the *Granth* teachings contrary to the *Qur'an*, the sixth Guru surrounded himself with bodyguards. Thus the military tradition of the Sikhs was begun.

The last Guru, Gobind Singh, organized the Sikhs for war. He introduced stories of Durga, the dreadful Hindu goddess of death, established the Granth as the final word for Sikhs (hence no more gurus), and developed the warrior class of the Singhs.

BELIEFS AND CHARACTERISTICS:

- Three Sects:
    1. Udasis – Ascetic holy men
    2. Sahajdharis – reject the militant trappings of most Sikhs
    3. Singhs – no stimulants, open to all castes, incredible warriors

- One God – "The True Name"

- No idols

- Reincarnation

- No caste system

- Meats are included in their diet.

- Originally pacifists, now *very* warlike

- Baptism is sprinkling a person with sweetened water when one reaches maturity.

- Daily rituals include morning bath, hymns, and prayers.

- Congregational worship:
    o Visiting the temple (Gurdwaras)
    o Prayer to the *Granth*
    o Hymns
    o Sermons
    o Communal meal
    o There is no priesthood
    o Men and women worship together

HUMANITY:

God's supreme creation and thus free to kill and eat animals. Man's spirit is reincarnated in men until "The True Name" frees them from this cycle.

LOCATION:

India and Indian communities around the world, but mainly in the Punjab region of northwest India.

SAYINGS OF SIKHISM

"By hearing the Name a blind man findeth his way. By hearing the Name the unfathomable becometh fathomable."

"Courtesy pointeth out the way that leadeth to God. The discourteous are beyond God's kindness."

"I have no anxiety regarding death, and I have no desire for life."

"God will not ask man of what race he is. He will ask what he has done."

"No one can erase what is written on the forehead."

"Great is the greatness of him who gives without being asked."

"He who knows himself will comprehend God."

"Many millions search for God and find him in their hearts."

"It is God who arrangeth marriages – those whom he hath once joined he joineth forever."

"I am not good, nor do I find anyone bad."

"Deem the body in which there is not love a place of cremation."

"The Name is a medicine for all diseases."

"By hearing the Name sorrow and sin are no more."

"Treat others as you would be treated yourself."

"The way of Sikhism is narrow: it is sharper than the edge of a sword and finer than a hair."

"The world is all made out of one clay, but the potter fashioned it into vessels of many sorts."

(The quotations above were taken from *The Eleven Religions and Their Proverbial Lore* by Selwyn G. Champion.)

TAOISM

(Pronounced Dow-ism)
(c. 2.6 million adherents)

FOUNDER:

Li Poh Yang, known as Lao Tzu ("Old Master"), 604-517 B.C.

GOD(S):

Originally the impersonal "Way" or "Tao", this belief system later developed into a religion with many gods.

All gods evolved from the flow of the Tao. The Tao is not thought of as a force that one can pray or sacrifice to. All one can do is live and flow with the Tao.

SCRIPTURES:

The *Tao Te Ching* (pronounced "dow-duh-jeang" and meaning "The Classic of the Way and Its Power.").

Tao Te Ching, could alternatively be translated as "Way Intelligence Book", or "A Book About Nature and Its Intelligent Life". "Tao" means "way," "path" or "road," and refers to the basic, primeval, ultimate nature of the cosmos. "Te" means "intelligence" or "integrity". Together, these terms could be describing acting in a natural, intelligent way, the power of Nature (since Nature is the source of everything, and everything has its own proper nature, then every action in accord with one's proper nature exhibits Te), and/or of being in harmony with Nature and thus finding inner peace. The basic theme of the book is that all achievements of people are folly, particularly elaborate government.

Legend says Lao Tzu wrote it as he waited to be allowed to leave China. Scholars believe it developed over the centuries and reached its present form in the fourth century B.C.

HISTORY:

Lao Tzu, keeper of the royal archives in the court of the Chou dynasty retired from his post and headed west to escape the complex life of the court. Having a reputation for being wise and scholarly, the philosopher was stopped by a border guard and not permitted to leave China until he had set his wisdom down in writing. Lao Tzu wrote the *Tao Te Ching*, was allowed to leave, and disappeared into the west. It is unknown if this story is true.

Early Taoists, such as Chuang Tzu, the fourth century B.C. disciple of Lao Tzu, were philosophers and intellectuals. They concerned themselves with living this life in a serene manner rather than with strong beliefs regarding gods, religion, or life after death. It appealed to a small group of people who were discontented with the complexities of society.

Later Taoism developed a second branch – one of scholars and magicians. In seeking for endless extension of this present life by being properly attuned to the Tao and alchemy, they began to worship gods. Mahayana Buddhism and Taoism struggled with each other in China during the first millennium, but eventually coalesced into close association.

BELIEFS AND CHARACTERISTICS:

A) Philosophical Taoism

- The basic unifying force behind the universe is the mysterious Tao.

- Life is the greatest of all possessions.

- Live life simply – despise pomp and glory.

- Religion of "trying to do nothing without being degenerate."

- *Yin Yang*: All things in nature and society are composed of Yin and Yang in different combinations.

    o Yin – dark, passive, female, negative, earth, moon, north, black. In Taoism, the Yin is emphasized.
    o Yang – bright, active, positive, masculine, heaven, sun, south, red.

- *Wu Wei*: let it happen, flow with the Tao – like breathing softly and having a blank mind.

- Unconcerned with strict morals: one should act according to circumstances.

- Doing what comes naturally.

- Admiration for ravines and valleys (not mountains), water and an uncarved block of wood. Water seems to illustrate seeking the lowest level as it flows around, over, under or through objects in its path.

- If the Tao is strong in one's life, one has no need for rules and regulations.

- The Tao – possible definitions:

    o Ultimate reality.
    o The way of the universe.
    o The way man can order his life.
    o Cannot be defined.

- To achieve the Tao – one must cleanse himself of impure thoughts and selfishness.

- Taijitu (Yin-Yang) as the symbol of Taoism.

An explanation of the various aspects and their meanings would be as follows:

- o Roundness – stands for Heaven and Nature
- o The Circle is an infinite symbol (like a wedding band), without beginning or end. It represents the singleness and all-embracing Nature of the universe.
- o Divided into two equal parts, representing the dual nature of the Tao (Yin/Yang). Also, the dividing line is not straight, but curved: nothing in Nature is simple. Just as different aspects of Nature (day and night, good and bad) phase into each other, so do the Yin/Yang teardrops. This shows the interlocking complexity of things, all of which are in constant state of flux.
- o Colors: one black and the other red – the Black/Yin and Red/Yang.
- o Each half has a spot of the other color in it: there is no such thing as pure Yin or Yang.

B) Popular Taoism

- Concerned with magic and alchemy (miracles).
- Worship the dead.
- Many gods.
- Monks and nuns. There is even a Taoist "pope" (who lives in Taiwan now).
- Seek to extend this life through magic.
- Religion of the masses.
- Heavens and hells.

HUMANITY:

This present life can be endlessly extended by being properly attuned to the Tao.

LOCATION:

China and Chinese communities throughout the world.

SAYINGS OF TAOISM

"The way that can be spoken of is not the constant way; the name that can be named is not the constant name."

"Thus Something and Nothing produce each other;
The difficult and the easy complement each other;
The long and the short off-set each other;
The high and the low incline towards each other;
Note and sound harmonize with each other;
Before and after follow each other."

"Therefore the sage keeps to the deed that consists in taking no action and practices the teaching that uses no words."

"Do that which consists in taking no action, and order will prevail."

"Much speech leads inevitably to silence. Better to hold fast to the void."

"The spirit of the valley never dies. This is called the mysterious female."

"Highest good is like water. Because water excels in benefiting the myriad creatures without contending with them and settles where none would like to be, it comes close to the way."

"To be overbearing when one has wealth and position is to bring calamity upon oneself. To retire when the task is accomplished is the way of heaven."

—

"And the people must have something to which they can attach themselves:

Exhibit the unadorned and embrace the uncarved block, have little thought of self and as few desires as possible."

"Between yea and nay how much difference is there? Between good and evil how great is the distance?"

"As a thing the way is shadowy, indistinct.
Indistinct and shadowy, yet within it is an image;
Shadowy and indistinct, yet within it is a substance.
Dim and dark, yet within it is an essence."

"The way never acts yet nothing is left undone."

"There is no crime greater than having too many desires; There is no disaster greater than not being content; There is no misfortune greater than being covetous."

"Governing a large state is like boiling a small fish."

"Beautiful words when offered will win high rank in return; Beautiful deeds can raise a man above others."

"The way of heaven excels in overcoming though it does not contend, in responding though it does not speak, in attracting though it does not summon, in laying plans though it appears slack."

(The quotations above were taken from *Tao Te Ching* by Lao Tzu.)

CONFUCIANISM

(c. 6.3 million adherents)

FOUNDER:

Ch'iu K'ung or Kung Fu-tse ("Kung the Master," commonly known in English as Confucius) who lived from 551 B.C. to 479 B.C.

GOD(S):

Traditional Chinese gods and ancestors are respected; there is even a cult around Confucius himself.

Ideally one should respect the spirits but keep them at a distance (Analects 6:20). Gods are not considered important and thus are not mentioned.

SCRIPTURES:

The Analects – the collection of Confucius' writings

HISTORY:

The feudal states of China were in decline by the sixth century B.C., leading up to the century of the warring states. The problem of social cohesion was on people's minds. Into this world Ch'iu K'ung was born. He was the youngest child of a poor family. He excelled in his schooling. He mastered the "six arts" of Rituals, Music, Archery, Calligraphy, Numerics and Charioteering. Confucius is an anglicized version of K'ung Fu Tse ("Master K'ung"). He was indeed a master, and was recognized in his late teens as a storehouse of knowledge and wisdom. Students came from all over to learn at his feet. Master K'ung was virtually a one-man university. He required diligence from all students as he taught. He once said, "Rotten wood cannot be carved" in reference to a lazy student.

Confucius loved tradition and the ancients. He taught his disciples a love for poetry and tradition, devotion and courage, honor and justice. Later he became a minister of justice in the government of the Duke of Lu. Confucius believed that man was basically good and that proper education would solve his ills. He experimented with the criminals in prison by doing a study of them and their educational levels. Then he began a program of teaching them correct principles of life. He also denounced the unjust judges and their corrupt practices of perverting judgment by showing favoritism to the rich and condemning the poor. After a few years, the prisons were empty. However, Confucius had made political enemies by his bold programs and denunciations. He was soon deposed and wandered about until given a position as the adviser of the Duke of Ai, which he held until his death.

Confucius' teachings were perpetuated by a small group of disciples until the fourth century B.C. Meng K'o (Mencius) lived from 372-289 B.C. and greatly reinforced Confucius' teachings. Hsun Tzu, 298-238 B.C., was a more unorthodox interpreter of Confucian Philosophy.

Shortly after Hsun Tzu, the Han dynasty arose and made a strong, well-governed China. Confucians were placed in charge of the education of Chinese youth. This is how, from 136 B.C. until 1905 A.D., Chinese education included the study of the teachings of Confucianism. Confucius bequeathed to the Chinese people a quest for knowledge, a love for family, and a respect for the elderly and tradition.

Recently, after years of antagonism, the Chinese communist government publicly celebrated the 2,535th anniversary of Confucius' birth.

BELIEFS AND CHARACTERISTICS:

- Living the best life now through a system of ethics.

- Goal – to become a Chun-Tzu "superior man," "man for all seasons," and ideal or wise person who is able to always do the right thing at the right time. A superior man follows these principles:

- o Li -- courtesy, propriety, expressing yourself in a kind and sincere manner, reduces friction in society
- o Yi -- duty, proper conduct, encouraging others to also be good
- o Jen -- human heartedness, goodwill, wanting to do what is best in the situation
- o Chih -- knowledge, wisdom (understand the world [Tao], how to act properly [Yi], being kind [Jen], behaving properly [Li])
- o Hsaio -- filial piety (honor parents)
- o Shu -- the silver rule
- o Cheng Ming -- sincerity

- "Silver Rule" – Don't do to others what you wouldn't want them to do to you.

- Confucius and Mencius believed in the basic goodness of man: if the environment were proper, people would naturally be virtuous.

- Hsun Tzu believed that a man is evil, but goodness can come through training, laws, and restraints.

- Confucius had a sense of mission on behalf of "Heaven", although he considered the gods as being rather impersonal.

- The best life found by man in human tradition and society – the good life is not beyond man.

- Ju-Chia – the philosophy of Confucianism. It teaches a form of practical morality and human relations. Ju-Chia was designed to provide the underpinnings for moral conduct of government, society and family. Officially it was the basis of Chinese civilization for 2000 years.

  K'ung Chiao – the Confucian religion. In this form, the religion was a state cult.

HUMANITY:

Basically good; if he does not act good it is because of the environment.

LOCATION:

China and Chinese communities around the world.

SAYINGS OF CONFUCIANISM

"The superior man seeks what is right, the inferior one what is profitable."

"Better than the one who knows what is right, is he who loves what is right."

"If a man can subdue his selfishness for one full day, everyone will call him good."

"When you leave your house, go out as if to meet an important guest."

"The superior man will be agreeable even when he disagrees; the inferior man will be disagreeable even when he agrees."

"The Master said, I do not see what use a man can be put to, whose word cannot be trusted. How can a wagon be made to go if it has no yoke-bar or a carriage, if it has no collar-bar?"

"The Master said, Just as to sacrifice to ancestors other than one's own is presumption, so to see what is right and not do it is cowardice."

"The Master said, High office filled by men of narrow views, ritual performed without reverence, the forms of mourning observed without grief – these are things I cannot bear to see!"

"The Master said, Without Goodness a man cannot for long endure adversity, cannot for long enjoy prosperity."

"Of the adage 'Only a Good Man knows how to like people, knows how to dislike them,' the Master said, He whose heart is in the smallest degree set upon Goodness will dislike no one."

"The Master said, He (the gentleman) does not mind not being in office; all he minds about is whether he has qualities that entitle him to office. He does not mind failing to get recognition; he is too busy doing the things that entitle him to recognition."

"The Master said, In the presence of a good man think all the time how you may learn to equal him. In the presence of a bad man, turn your gaze within!"

"The Master said, in serving his father and mother a man may gently remonstrate with them. But if he sees that he has failed to change their opinion, he should resume an attitude of deference and not thwart them; may feel discouraged, but not resentful."

"The Master said, A gentleman covets the reputation of being slow in word but prompt in deed."

"When in the Master's presence anyone sang a song that he liked, he did not join in at once, but asked for it to be repeated and then joined in."

"The Master's manner was affable yet firm, commanding but not harsh, polite but easy."

"The Master said, Only when men of the right sort have instructed a people for seven years ought there to be any talk of engaging them in warfare. The Master said, To lead into battle a people that has not first been instructed is to betray them."

(The quotations above were taken from the *Analects of Confucius* by Arthur Waley and from *What the Great Religions Believe* by Joseph Gaer.)

SHINTOISM

(c. 2.8 million adherents)

FOUNDER:

None

GOD(S):

Many gods (called "Kami") are worshipped (there are 1,550 Kami listed in one source). The emperors of Japan are considered descendants of Amateratsu, the sun goddess.

SCRIPTURES:

Kojiki ("Chronicle of Ancient Events"); *Nihon Shoki* ("Chronicles of Japan")

HISTORY:

Prior to the coming of Buddhism to Japan in the sixth century A.D., Japanese religion was a varied collection of practices. As Buddhism, Confucianism and Taoism began to influence the Japanese, the *Kojiki* was written to preserve the indigenous Shinto religion. The distinctions between Shinto and Japanese Mahayana Buddhism have largely faded. Concerns of day-to-day life are Shinto; concerns for the afterlife are Buddhist.

During the Tokugawa period (1600-1867 A.D.) the military rulers encouraged Shinto and other religions were largely suppressed. Even after the opening of Japan by Commodore Perry in 1854, the Japanese government supported Shinto. After the Second World War, the Allied occupation forces ended emperor worship and the political side of Shinto.

Today, the religious side of Shinto is represented by sects worshipping mountains, such as Tenri-Kyo (Shamanistic faith healing, "the Christian Science of Japan"), and pure Shinto (which emphasizes the purification of the body).

BELIEFS AND CHARACTERISTICS:

- They believe the first emperor of Japan, Jimmu Tenno, was descended from Amateratsu, the sun goddess and chief Kami.

- Izanagi and his wife, Izanami, are the creators of the Japanese Islands and are the parents of all the Kami.

- Happy, joyful, bright, beautiful are areas with which Shinto concerns itself.

- A deep love of nature. Sunrise is a favorite theme in Shinto poetry.

- Nationalistic.

- Personal, private worship – many Japanese homes have a Kami-Dana (god shelf) in them where any objects they consider sacred are kept. Simple daily offerings and prayers are made here. In addition to their Kami-Dana, many homes also have a Butsu-Dan, a Buddhist household altar, in case another form of religious occasion is needed.

- Temples have no idols or images; are for prayer and offerings.

- Shinto is a Chinese word that means "way of the gods." The name in Japanese is Kami-No-Michi.

- Life is good.

- Good deeds are more important than mere words.

- All natural desires are good unless taken to excess.

- The Samurai Code of Behavior:

- o Courage – blind loyalty.
- o Cowardice – unforgivable sin; they prefer death to dishonor.
- o Loyalty – to emperor, family, community, and future generations.
- o Cleanliness – bathing, purification.

HUMANITY:

Shinto is a nature-culture religion in which man tries to fit in as best he can through rituals and actions. Primary concern is living life now. In Shinto, there is not much thought about afterlife. There is a belief in Shinto writings that the Japanese are a special people since they came from the gods – particularly Amaterasu, the sun goddess.

LOCATION:

Japan

SAYINGS OF SHINTOISM

"Both heaven and hell come from one's own heart."

"All men are brothers; all receive the blessings of the same heaven."

"With God there is neither day nor night, neither far nor near."

"Do not profess love with your lips while you harbor hatred in your heart."

"One should not be mindful of suffering in his own life and unmindful of suffering in the lives of others."

"In all the world there is no such thing as a stranger."

(The quotations above were taken from *What the Great Religions Believe* by Joseph Gaer.)

ZOROASTRIANISM

(c. 174 thousand adherents)

FOUNDER:

Zarathustra (Zoroaster) Spitama (c. 660-583 B.C.)

GOD(S):

Ahura Mazda, the distant high god worshipped by the Aryans for centuries, was declared to be the only god by Zoroaster. However, Zoroastrianism is often referred to as dualistic because besides Ahura Mazda as the good god, there is also the evil god Angra Mainyu struggling against him.

SCRIPTURES:

Zend-Avesta (Especially the *Gathas* – the hymns of early Zoroastrianism, which are looked upon as being Zoroaster's very words.)

HISTORY:

Zoroaster, considered the last and greatest of the sashyants (prophets or reformers) of Persia, was born into a wealthy family. It is said he had 3 wives and 6 children. At age 30, he was pondering disturbing theological questions when an angel from Ahura Mazda appeared to him and commissioned him to be his prophet. Over the next ten years he had other visions, but was unable to convert anyone. Finally his cousin was converted. Soon thereafter, he went to the court of a Bactrian king named Vishtaspa, stayed in his court for several years and eventually converted Vishtaspa and his courtiers (apparently they were overjoyed when the king's favorite horse was healed by Zoroaster). Zoroastrianism spread rapidly after this occasion. An enemy soldier killed Zoroaster at age 77.

Perhaps the Persian king Cyrus was a Zoroastrian; Darius certainly worshipped Ahura Mazda. But, it was not until the period of the Sassanid Rulers (226-642 A.D.) that Zoroastrianism became the only official religion of Persia. After that, the Muslim invasions virtually stamped Zoroastrianism out by the ninth century. Zoroastrianism is today almost extinct, with the largest remaining communities being the Parsees (the descendants of ancient Persian immigrants) in North Western India.

BELIEFS AND CHARACTERISTICS:

- After death the soul goes to heaven or hell (depending on the balance of good or bad deeds). They are there to be rewarded or punished until the end of the world. Then, all will be resurrected and purified and live together in righteousness. Angra Mainyu and his demons will be destroyed and a new world will be created.

- Sacred Elements:

    o Earth
    o Fire
    o Water
    o Air

- Ethics: Good thought, good word, good deed. Zoroastrians are still known for their purity, honesty, and concern for their children.

- Worship:

    o Prayers
    o Offer sandalwood to sacred flames
    o Rites of passage
    o At death the body is not buried but instead is placed in a "Tower of Silence" so that the elements will not be defiled.

HUMANITY:

Man has free will and can choose to cast his lot in this life with the force of evil or of good. Individuals are considered totally free to make their own choices for which they will be held accountable. If people live ethically, it is felt the ultimate destiny of the world will be better.

"Evil to evil, good to good," the law of retribution, of cause and effect is taught. This is carried to such extreme that there is no means of atonement for evil deeds.

LOCATION:

Approximately 11,000 "Gabars" (infidels) continue to live in Iran. Another 100,000 live in India (mostly in Bombay) and the rest are scattered in small communities around the world.

SAYINGS OF ZOROASTRIANISM

"We worship Ahura Mazda who made the kine and the righteousness ... and the waters, and the wholesome plants, the stars, and the earth, and all existing objects that are good."

"Let no thought of Angra Mainyu (the devil) ever infect thee, so that thou should indulge in evil lusts, make derision and idolatry, and shut (to the poor) the door of thy house."

"Of two bed-fellows who hear the cock crowing, the one who gets up first will first enter paradise."

"The dead shall rise up, life shall come back to the bodies and they shall keep the breath."

"He is evil who is best to the evil, and he is holy to whom the holy is a friend."

"To live in fear and falsehood is worse than death."

"The first perfection is good thoughts, the second good words, and the third good deeds."

"That nature only is good when it shall not do unto another whatever is not good for its own self."

"Do not unto others all that which is not well for oneself."

"Poverty which is through honesty is better than opulence which is from the treasure of others."

"One truthful man is better than the whole world speaking falsehood."

(The quotations above were taken from *The Eleven Religions and Their Proverbial Lore* by Selwyn G. Champion.)

JUDAISM

(c. 14 million adherents)

FOUNDER:

No single Founder, although Moses is usually credited.

GOD(S):

YHVH

SCRIPTURES:

Tanakh (Law [*Torah* - the oldest and most revered part of the *Tanakh*], Prophets and Writings collected in the Bible) also simply called *Holy Scriptures*. Christians refer to this part of the *Holy Bible* as "The Hebrew Scriptures" or "The Old Testament."

Talmud – Commentary considered to be a collection of the "Oral Law" which was completed about 500 A.D. the *Talmud* includes both the *Mishnah* (a commentary on the Pentateuch) and the *Gemara* (a commentary about the *Mishnah*). The Babylonian edition of the *Talmud* is considered the more authoritative, although the Palestinian edition of the *Talmud* is older.

HISTORY:

According to the *Holy Scriptures*, God made Adam and Eve in the beginning as the first human beings. To them and their family He gave His law and instructions. When they sinned, God closed up the Tree of Life and cast them out of the Garden of Eden. Future generations became corrupt so God had to destroy mankind at the Flood. He saved only Noah and his family. After the flood there were some righteous people such as Abraham and Sarah and some of their descendants. In time, some of these descendants became slaves in Egypt.

All Israelites were called out of Egypt from slavery by God. They promised to obey God and be an example. They did not succeed. First they split into two kingdoms after Solomon: the state of Israel (the "Ten Tribes") to the north, and the state of Judah to the south. Then they ceased observing God's laws. Eventually, both states went into captivity. Israel first in 721 B.C. and then Judah in 587 B.C.

The Ten Tribes disappeared from history, but the Jews maintained their identity and tried to get back to sincerely practicing their religion. After their return from 70 years of captivity in Mesopotamia, the Jews began to add interpretations to the laws of Moses. These interpretations were set down in the *Talmud*, and were explained to be an "oral law" to be considered in addition to the "written law" of the *Holy Scriptures*.

In later centuries, the Jews were scattered and persecuted from the fall of Jerusalem to the Roman armies in 70 A.D., until the establishment of the Jewish state of Israel in 1948.

BELIEFS AND CHARACTERISTICS:

- First religion to teach one God.

- Deep reverence for the Law (Torah).

- A Jew is a person from an ethnic Jewish background who is also connected by religious ties to the Jewish faith and is born of a Jewish mother.

- Two Basic Cultural Groups of Judaism today:
    - o Ashkenazim – Jews whose ancestors lived in northern and Eastern Europe.
    - o Sephardic – Jews whose ancestors lived in Spain, Portugal, and the Middle East.

- A convert is not just to the religion. One must also accept the community of Israel.

- Land of Israel is important to the Jews for its historic and future value. There are many references to the land of Israel and the city of Jerusalem in the Scriptures. Many customs and ceremonies are still attached to this geographical area.

- Two key practices: Sabbath and circumcision.

- Their mission is as a chosen people who will eventually be vindicated (Ezekiel 37).

- Justice and truth are important virtues.

- Tends to have more individual worship than group worship.

- Bar Mitzvah – ceremony at which a boy becomes a man or "Son of the Covenant" at age 13 (in Reform Judaism, there is a corresponding Bat Mitzvah for girls).

- Jewish Parties during the life of Jesus Christ:

  o Sadducees: Wealthy, aristocratic, were concerned with politics. Believed in the *written* word only. Were compromising and would culturally accept the views of the times. Disappeared after conquest of Jerusalem by Romans in 70 A.D.
  o Pharisees: "Puritan" types; non-compromising. Scribes, Rabbis and lower orders of priests formed this party. They believed in the resurrection and the future Messiah.
  o Herodians: Supported the house of Herod. Wanted home rule at any cost. Disappeared after conquest of Jerusalem by Romans in 70 A.D.
  o Zealots: Rebels against Rome's domination. Believed that submission to Rome was against God's will. They thought fighting would be pleasing to God and perhaps induce the coming of the Messiah. Annihilated during conquest of Judah by Romans in 70 AD.
  o Essenes: A communal group who withdrew from society. Shared meals and goods. They observed

the Sabbath with extreme strictness. Their view was to be non-violent and "wait for God" to work things out. Annihilated during conquest of Judah by Romans in 70 A.D.

- Basic Groups Today:

    o Reform Judaism: Liberal movement. They reject revelation, but rather they look upon the Torah as a source of ethics.
    o Conservative Judaism: Take the law seriously as a guide to life. Can alter some teachings of law and tradition to suit modern times.
    o Orthodox Judaism: The Torah is literal and divine as revelation and cannot be changed.
    o Ultra-Orthodox: The "Hasidim" are even more fervent in practicing their religion than even the Orthodox.

- Thirteen Articles of Faith:

    1. God is the Creator
    2. There is only one God – monotheism
    3. God is incorporeal – doesn't have a body
    4. God is Eternal
    5. God alone must be worshipped
    6. The inspiration of the prophets
    7. Moses was the greatest of the prophets
    8. The entire law was divinely given to Moses
    9. The law is immutable and permanent
    10. God is omniscient – knows everything
    11. There are rewards and punishments – a divine plan being worked out
    12. The coming of the Messiah (only the Orthodox await Him – others reinterpret this belief)
    13. Resurrection of the Just and Unjust

(From: *Guide to the Perplexed* by Moses Maimonides)

HUMANITY:

Responsible to live the way of the Torah. Made in the image of God, all humans have a spirit in them (a Yetzer) that is inclined to evil and must be mastered. It can be mastered through one's own efforts in prayer, study, good deeds and habitually doing right. The immortal soul of a person at death goes to the Maker if good and to hell if evil, to be cleansed. Ultimately all go to the Maker.

Most Jews concentrate on living in the present with little vision of afterlife.

LOCATION:

The world's largest national Jewish communities:

United States	5.8 million
Israel	3.1 million
USSR	2.6 million
France	650,000
United Kingdom	410,000
Canada	305,000
Argentina	300,000

SAYINGS OF JUDAISM

"He who performs a single good action gains for himself an advocate; he who commits a single sin, procures for himself an accuser."

"Man must bless God in his affliction as well as in his joy."

"Loans are preferable to alms giving."

"When the wise is angry he is wise no longer."

"We generally reproach others with blemishes similar to our own."

"He who gives charity in secret is greater than Moses himself."

"The chastisements of God are afflictions of love."

"Cleanliness is next to godliness."

"One loose cord loosens many."

"No man is impatient with his creditors."

"Custom is law."

"The end does not justify the means."

"Make a fence to thy words."

"He who is loved by man is loved by God."

"Before God, a good intention is as the deed."

"Everything lies in the hand of God save the fear of God."

"The heart that loves is always young."

"Who practices hospitality entertains God himself."

"All Israelites have a portion in the world to come."

"Love the poor that thy children may not come to poverty."

"Prayer is worship in the heart."

"Truth is heavy, therefore few care to carry it."

"Ten measures of speech descended to the world; women took nine and men one."

"Work honors the workman."

"Hear, 0 Israel: the Lord our God, the Lord is one." (Known as the "Shemah" ["Hear"], from Deuteronomy 6:4)

"And thou shalt love the Lord thy god with all thy heart, and with all thy soul, and with all thy might. And these words, which I command thee this day, shall be upon thy heart; and thou shalt teach them diligently unto thy children, and shalt talk of them when thou sittest in thy house, and when thou walkest by the way, and when thou liest down, and when thou risest up. And thou shalt bind them for a sign upon thy hand, and they shall be for frontlets between thine eyes. And thou shalt write them upon the door-posts of thy house, and upon thy gates." (Deuteronomy 6:5-9)

"Ye have seen what I did unto the Egyptians, and how I bore you on eagles' wings, and brought you unto Myself. Now therefore, if ye will hearken unto My voice indeed, and keep My covenant, then ye shall be Mine own treasure from among all peoples; for all the earth is Mine; and ye shall be unto Me a kingdom of priests, and a holy nation. These are the words which thou shalt speak unto the children of Israel!" (Exodus 19:4-6)

"And God spoke all these words, saying:

"I am the Lord thy God, who brought thee out of the land of Egypt, out of the house of bondage.

"Thou shalt have no other gods before Me. Thou shalt not make unto thee a graven image, nor any manner of likeness, of any thing that is in heaven above, or that is in the earth beneath, or that is in the water under the earth; thou shalt not bow down unto them, nor serve them; for I the Lord thy God am a jealous God, visiting the iniquity of the fathers upon the children unto the third and fourth generation of them that hate Me; and showing mercy unto the thousandth generation of them that love Me and keep My commandments.

"Thou shalt not take the name of the Lord thy God in vain; for the Lord will not hold him guiltless that taketh His name in vain.

"Remember the Sabbath day, to keep it holy. Six days shalt thou labour, and do all thy work; but the seventh day is a Sabbath unto the Lord thy God, in it thou shalt not do any manner of work, thou, nor thy son, nor thy daughter, nor thy man-servant, nor thy maid-servant, nor thy cattle, nor thy stranger that is within thy gates; for in six days the Lord made heaven and earth, the sea, and all that in them is, and rested on the seventh day; wherefore the Lord blessed the Sabbath day, and hallowed it.

"Honour thy father and thy mother, that thy days may be long upon the land which the Lord thy God giveth thee.

"Thou shalt not murder.

"Thou shalt not commit adultery.

"Thou shalt not steal.

"Thou shalt not bear false witness against thy neighbour.

"Thou shalt not covet thy neighbour's house; thou shalt not covet thy neighbour's wife, nor his man-servant, nor his maid-servant, nor his ox, nor his ass, nor any thing that is thy neighbour's." (Exodus 20:1-17)

"And it shall come to pass in the end of days, that the mountain of the Lord's house shall be established as the top of the mountains, and shall be exalted above the hills; and all nations shall flow unto it. And many peoples shall go and say: 'come ye, and let us go up to the mountain of the Lord, to the house of the God of Jacob; and He will teach us of His ways, and we will walk in His paths.' For out of Zion shall go forth the law and the word of the Lord from Jerusalem. And He shall judge between the nations, and shall decide for many peoples; and they shall beat their swords into plowshares, and their spears into pruning-hooks; nation shall not lift up sword against nation, neither shall they learn war any more." (Isaiah 2:2-4)

"Thus saith the Lord of hosts: I am jealous for Zion with great jealousy, and I am jealous for her with great fury. Thus saith the Lord: I return unto Zion, and will dwell in the midst of Jerusalem; and Jerusalem shall be called the city of truth; and the mountain of the Lord of hosts the holy mountain." (Zechariah 8:2-3)

(The quotations above were taken from *The Eleven Religions and Their Proverbial Lore* by Selwyn G. Champion and from *The Holy Scriptures* by the Jewish Publication Society of America.)

CHRISTIANITY

(See Section II for Various Christian Denominations)
(over 2 billion adherents)

FOUNDER:

Jesus Christ (c. 4 B.C. – c. 31 A.D.)

GOD(S):

Usually a belief in one God of three persons – the Trinity.

SCRIPTURES:

The Holy Bible is usually taken as the Word of God.

HISTORY:

Jesus Christ, a Jew, preached a new way of life to the world. The New Testament writings record him as being the Son of God, one who brought the spiritual intent of the law (*Torah*) and also became the ultimate sacrifice to provide grace and forgiveness. After his execution by the Romans, his disciples saw him resurrected and, as he had told them, went on to proclaim his gospel message to the world, and to teach his followers who were to come from all nations.

After several years of preaching in Jerusalem, the disciples suffered persecution at the hands of the Jews. Christianity at first looked like a Jewish sect. Soon, it became apparent that it was not. Periods of official Roman persecution took place against this new, unrecognized religion. Saul of Tarsus was a chief persecutor of the infant church until he converted to Christianity when confronted by the resurrected Jesus on the road to Damascus. Changing his name to Paul, he later became the apostle of the Gentiles and took the gospel to Europe. The original disciples did their utmost to reach the inhabited world with God's message. Numerical and spiritual growth took place.

As the first century A.D. came to a close, the Church underwent considerable change. Persecutions and the influence of the surrounding pagan society caused Christianity to appear less and less outwardly like a Jewish sect, and many new practices were adopted by a majority of Christians. During the Second Jewish Revolt (c. 130 A.D.) most Christians began to avoid many practices considered Jewish. Over the next few centuries Christianity gradually became the major religion of the Roman Empire, and later converted the Barbarian Kingdoms that overthrew Rome.

In 1054 A.D. a split took place between the West and the East with Roman Catholicism becoming a separate Church in the West and Eastern Orthodox in the East. The rift was widened and sealed by the sacking of Constantinople in 1204 A.D. by the Crusaders from the West.

After the Black Death Plague of 1347-1351, many began to question their religion. Just over one hundred years later Martin Luther (1483-1546), a Catholic Priest and Professor challenged the Catholic Church on its teaching regarding selling indulgences (in effect "selling forgiveness") and also the authority of the Pope. Thus, in the years following his posting of the 95 Thesis in 1517 (see Lutheranism below), began the Protestant Reformation. Soon England also became protestant and John Calvin, a Frenchman, built Geneva into a Protestant stronghold. The work of Knox, Wesley, Zwingli and others solidified the revolt of the Protestants. Today there are well over 500 different denominations, sects and cults all professing Christianity.

BELIEFS AND CHARACTERISTICS:

There are a wide variety of beliefs in Christianity. Specific denominational beliefs are covered later in this book. The following are some general ones.

- Jesus Christ is the Son of God and Savior of the world. He was God and man. Note: Jesus Christ is the anglicized form of the Greek for "Joshua the Messiah".

- God is a trinity (one God composed of three persons: Father, Son and Holy Spirit).

- Baptism and Lord's Supper (Communion or Eucharist) are essential to most denominations. (Catholics and Orthodox have Seven Sacraments including these two.)

- Confirmation by laying on of hands.

- *The Holy Bible* is the Word of God.

- Salvation is the gift of God.

- A Christian is under grace - unmerited help and forgiveness from God.

- The Ten Commandments should be the basis of Christian morality – with denominational interpretations.

- Usually observe Sunday as the day of worship.

- Most believe in the resurrection of the body at the judgment.

- The return of Jesus Christ prior to the Day of Judgment.

- The need to spread the teachings of Jesus Christ.

- Love your God and love your neighbor sums up the law of God.

- Original sin - all people are born sinful because of the first sin of Adam and Eve in the Garden of Eden.

- Religious freedom.

- Most protestant churches emphasize faith and not works.

- Prayer and study are important for spiritual growth.

- Nicene and Apostles' Creeds.

- Most denounce "worldliness," but interpretations of its meaning vary.

- Heaven for the saved and hell for the condemned.

HUMANITY:

Made in the image of God, humans are composed of a body and soul. At death the soul will be rewarded or punished. To be saved, the man must accept Jesus Christ as his savior, repent and be baptized and remain under grace to the end of his life. At death, the soul goes to its designated destiny (heaven or hell). At the final judgment the body will be resurrected to join the soul in happiness or punishment. Most churches teach that heaven is being in the presence of God for all eternity with good companions amidst happiness. Hell means punishment forever with sense of loss felt from being deprived of God's presence. The company of demons and sinners adds to the grief.

LOCATIONS:

Christianity has worldwide influence – particularly in Europe, the Americas, Australia/Oceana, Central and Southern Africa.

SAYINGS OF CHRISTIANITY

"In the beginning was the Word, and the Word was with God, and the Word was God. He was in the beginning with God . . . And the Word became flesh and dwelt among us, and we beheld His glory, the glory as of the only begotten of the Father, full of grace and truth." (John 1: 1-2, 14)

"For God so loved the world that He gave His only begotten Son, that whoever believes in Him should not perish but have everlasting life." (John 3:16)

"The thief does not come except to steal, and to kill, and to destroy. I have come that they may have life, and that they may have it more abundantly." (John 10:10)

"Therefore, whatever you want men to do to you, do also to them, for this is the Law and the Prophets." (Matthew 7:12)

"Jesus said to him, 'You shall love the Lord your God with all your heart, with all your soul, and with all your mind. This is the first and great commandment. And the second is like it: You shall love your neighbor as yourself.'" (Matthew 22:37-39)

"For we do not have a High Priest who cannot sympathize with our weaknesses, but was in all points tempted as we are, yet without sin. Let us therefore come boldly to the throne of grace, that we may obtain mercy and find grace to help in time of need." (Hebrews 4:15-16)

"My little children, these things I write to you, that you may not sin. And if anyone sins, we have an Advocate with the Father, Jesus Christ the righteous. And He Himself is the propitiation for our sins, and not for ours only, but also for the whole world." (I John 2:1-2)

"For by grace you have been saved through faith, and that not of yourselves; it is the gift of God, not of works, lest anyone should boast. For we are His workmanship, created in Christ Jesus for good works, which God prepared beforehand that we should walk in them." (Ephesians 2:8-10)

"And seeing the multitudes, He went up on a mountain and when He was seated His disciples came to Him. Then He opened His mouth and taught them, saying:

'Blessed are the poor in spirit, for theirs is the kingdom of heaven.

Blessed are those who mourn, for they shall be comforted.

Blessed are the meek, for they shall inherit the earth.

Blessed are those who hunger and thirst for righteousness, for they shall be filled.

Blessed are the merciful, for they shall obtain mercy.

Blessed are the pure in heart, for they shall see God.

Blessed are the peacemakers, for they shall be called sons of God.

Blessed are those who are persecuted for righteousness' sake, for theirs is the kingdom of heaven.

Blessed are you when they revile and persecute you, and say all kinds of evil against you falsely for my sake. Rejoice and be exceedingly glad, for great is your reward in heaven, for so they persecuted the prophets who were before you.'" (Matthew 5:1-12)

"Whoever commits sin also commits lawlessness, and sin is lawlessness." (I John 3:4)

"For this is the love of God, that we keep His commandments. And His commandments are not burdensome." (I John 5:3)

"Now this I say, brethren, that flesh and blood cannot inherit the kingdom of God; nor does corruption inherit incorruption." (I Corinthians 15:50-52)

"In this manner, therefore, pray:
Our Father in heaven, hallowed be Your name.
Your kingdom come.
Your will be done on earth as it is in heaven.
Give us this day our daily bread.
And forgive us our debts, as we forgive our debtors.
And do not lead us into temptation, but deliver us from the evil one.
For Yours is the kingdom and the power and the glory forever.
Amen." (Matthew 6:9-13)

"But the fruit of the Spirit is love, joy, peace, longsuffering, kindness, goodness, faithfulness, gentleness, self-control. Against such there is no law." (Galatians 5:22-23)

"And He said to them, 'Go into all the world and preach the gospel to every creature.'" (Mark 16:15)

"Then Peter said to them, 'Repent, and let every one of you be baptized in the name of Jesus Christ for the remission of sins; and you shall receive the gift of the Holy Spirit.'" (Acts 2:38)

"Pure and undefiled religion before God and the Father is this: to visit orphans and widows in their trouble, and to keep oneself unspotted from the world." (James 1:27)

"But do you want to know, O foolish man, that faith without works is dead?" (James 2:20)

"But you shall receive power when the Holy Spirit has come upon you; and you shall be witnesses to Me in Jerusalem, and in all Judea and Samaria, and to the end of the earth." (Acts 1:8)

(The quotations above were taken from the *The Holy Bible, the New King James Version*, by Thomas Nelson Publishers.)

ISLAM

(c. 1.3 Billion adherents)

FOUNDER:

Muhammad (c. 570-632 A.D.)

GOD(S):

Allah (the Arabic word for God). Creator, omnipresent, omnipotent, omniscient, sovereign over the entire universe.

SCRIPTURES:

The *Qur'an* (*Koran*) – means the "Reading." It is four-fifths the size of the New Testament and contains 114 Suras or divisions. Each Sura begins with "In the Name of Allah ...". The *Qur'an* is written in classical Arabic and contains the speeches and sermons of Muhammad. Each word is believed to be the word of God. The *Qur'an* emphasizes the Oneness of God though it tends to picture God as punishing people who do wrong. Submission to Allah and avoidance of "Shirk" or idolatry are emphasized. Human relationships are also expounded. The *Qur'an* is a unifying force in the Muslim world.

The Hadith, collections of stories of teachings and actions of Muhammad, are often referred to when trying to determine what a Muslim should do in situations. There are approximately 500,000 Hadith, averaging 3 paragraphs in length.

HISTORY:

Muhammad was raised by his uncle Abu-Talib, chief of the Quraysh tribe in the city of Mecca. He was illiterate and his occupation was a camel driver. As such, he traveled throughout the Middle East and was exposed to Judaism, Christianity, and Zoroastrianism. At 25, he married the 40-year-old owner of the caravan, Khadija, whose wealth gave him time to think out the theological questions he had. In 610 A.D., at the age of 40, he began to experience a series of visions and said that Allah through the angel Gabriel was talking to him by these visions.

He began to preach to the people of Mecca as Allah's prophet, speaking out against their multitudinous gods and idols. Needless to say, he was not well liked and eventually (622 A.D.) had to flee to the town of Yathrib (later renamed Medina). This flight was called the Hijrah (Hegira). Up until this point Muhammad's revelations and teaching had been to be tolerant toward others when persecuted, and that he was just a "plain warner". After moving to Medina, his revelations and teachings became more aggressive and military conquest was taught as the way to expand the faith. He became a ruler of men. After the death of Khadija, Mohammad married twelve women, and had twenty three female slaves. This is interpreted as being a development of revelation to Muhammad over time.

The Muslims in Medina warred against the Arabs in Mecca and the Jewish tribes of the desert, eventually overcoming them in 630. Muhammad died in 632. Islam expanded explosively until 732 when their conquests in the west were halted in France by Charles Martel at the Battle of Tours, and in the east in the fourteenth century when they were unable to make further penetration into India (later Indonesia and Malaysia were converted relatively peacefully during the course of the 15th and 16 th centuries). In the twentieth century Muslim missionary activity was rekindled, and today approximately one-third of Africa is Muslim.

BELIEFS AND CHARACTERISTICS:

- The *Qur'an* is the absolute word of God – eternal, absolute and irrevocable.

- There is only one God – Allah. Militant monotheism.

- Fatalism – Allah only allows people to make choices in areas they'll be judged, the rest is predetermined.

- Jesus, Moses, Abraham, and others were prophets of Allah, but Muhammad was the final prophet. Regard Jesus highly, but deny that he was the Son of God or was resurrected.

- The Five Pillars:

    1. "No other god but Allah, and his prophet is Muhammad."
    2. Ritual prayer five times a day towards Mecca.
    3. Fast during Ramadan.
    4. Alms giving (mandatory 2.5% of income).
    5. Pilgrimage to Mecca (Hajj) to see the cube of the Kaaba and its black meteorite stone.

- Seven Ruinous Sins:

    1. Associating anything with God.
    2. Using or dealing with Magic.
    3. Killing people without reason.
    4. Earning interest on money.
    5. Deserting the army when Jihad (holy war) is declared.
    6. Appropriating an orphan's property.
    7. Accusing a woman of adultery when she is innocent.

- Allah is not considered a father figure as in Christianity or Judaism, but a master to whom one must be submitted. Allah is stern towards people, particularly unbelievers.

- A Muslim is the slave of Allah who should treat other Muslims kindly, and spread Islam over the unbelievers by conversion or conquest.

- Do not eat pork or pork products.

- Legally, women in Islam have half the weight of a man in inheritances and as witnesses. In the *Qur'an* it is taught that women should be covered, which is today interpreted in various ways. In Islam it is acceptable for a man to divorce a woman under many circumstances. A Muslim man may have up to 4 wives, as long as he can support them.

- Jihad - "Holy War" - was taught by Muhammad to be waged against unbelievers for the spread of the faith and for reward to the faithful. Today, moderate Muslims interpret Jihad as struggling within yourself to do the right thing.

- A seasonally inaccurate lunar calendar (100 solar years = 103 Muslim years), i.e. months are unrelated to the seasons.

- Allah will judge all men at the end of time. No one can know before the judgment day if they have pleased Allah in this life or not - hope is in the shadow of doubt.

- Paradise is envisioned as a location with luxuries and abundance of food and wine. Beautiful virgins surround the righteous.

- Sunni's (85% of all Muslims, c. 1 billion adherents) are the conservative branch. Shiites (most of the remaining 15% of Muslims, c. 200 million adherents) believe in a coming Mahdi (Messiah), look for hidden meanings in the *Qur'an*, and believe that Allah's revelation didn't end with Muhammad but continues through "Imams" (Holy men).

HUMANITY:

In this life: "I created humankind only that they might worship me" – (*Qur'an*). No distinction made between worship and life itself. One's life is already pre-determined by Allah.

In the afterlife: When a man dies, his body goes back to the earth, but his soul sleeps until the resurrection. The angel of Allah will sound a trumpet, the earth will split and the resurrection will occur. Bodies and souls will be rejoined. Allah will then judge all by the *Qur'an*.

LOCATION:

Sunni: Northern Africa, Arabia, Turkey, Central Asia, Afghanistan, Pakistan, India, Indonesia, Bangladesh and northern and western Iraq. *Shiite*: Iran, Lebanon, part of eastern Saudi Arabia and southern and eastern Iraq.

SAYINGS OF ISLAM

"To Allah belongs the East and the West he guideth whom he willeth to a straight path."

"Ye cannot attain to righteousness until ye expend in alms of what ye love."

"Our God and your God is one, and to Him are we self surrendered (Muslims)."

"But he who is blind in this life will be blind in the hereafter and far astray from the way."

"This is guidance; and those who disbelieve in the signs of their Lord, there awaits them a painful chastisement of wrath." (*Qur'an* 5:10)

"Whoso does righteousness, it is to his own gain, and whoso does evil, it is to his own loss; then to your Lord you shall be returned." (*Qur'an* 45:14)

"Those only are believers, who believe in God and His messenger . .

(*Qur'an* 24:61)

"And who so slays a believer willfully, his recompense is Gehenna .

(*Qur'an* 4:95)

"Whatever good visits thee, it is of God; whatever evil visits thee is of thyself." (*Qur'an* 4:80)

God is All-forgiving, All-compassionate . . . All-knowing, All-wise." (*Qur'an* 4:10)

"Whatever good you do, God knows it." (*Qur'an* 2:194)

"And fight in the way of God with those who fight you, but aggress not. God loves not the aggressors." (*Qur'an* 2:187)

(The quotations above were taken from *The Eleven Religions and Their Proverbial Lore* by Selwyn G. Champion and *The Koran Interpreted* by A. J. Arberry.)

SECTION II

—

CHRISTIAN DENOMINATIONS

ROMAN CATHOLICISM

(c. 1 billion adherents)

FOUNDER:

Jesus Christ. Peter is highly honored as well as his successors, the Popes (who are considered the Vicars of Christ). Founded in c. 33 A.D.

GOD(S):

A trinity. Three persons in One; Father, Son and Holy Spirit are co-equal and co-eternal. This doctrine was officially formed in 325 A.D. at Council of Nicea, and codified at Council of Chalcedon in 51 A.D.

SCRIPTURES:

The *Holy Bible* and Tradition. The Catholic Bible contains seven extra books and additions to other books of the Orthodox and Protestant Bible.

HISTORY:

The Roman and Greek Orthodox churches were one until a rift developed over a clause in the creed regarding the procession of the Holy Spirit. The Roman Church said it proceeds from the Father *and* the Son. The Orthodox said *only* the Father gives it. The primacy of the Pope (Bishop of Rome) was also a source of division. The split was made final in 1054 A.D. when the Bishop of Rome and the Bishop of Constantinople excommunicated each other. It was reinforced in 1204 A.D. when Western (Roman) Christians sacked Constantinople.

Since the sixteenth century, the name "Roman Catholic" was applied to the body of individuals that acknowledges the Pope and looks to the leadership at Rome. Catholic means universal.

CHURCH ORGANIZATION:

- Hierarchal in form with the Pope being infallible when he rules on matters of doctrine and faith. He must state that he is speaking officially on these matters for infallibility to be in effect.

  They believe they are the One True Church because of the following:

  - One – unity of faith
  - Holy – God is in it
  - Apostolic – ordinations of bishops in succession from original apostles
  - Catholic – they are worldwide in scope and largest of all.

CREED:

Apostles' Creed (see Appendix 9)

CHARACTERISTICS:

- The Church is three-faceted:

  1. the Church Triumphant – souls in heaven
  2. the Church Expectant – souls in purgatory
  3. the Church militant – people on earth

  The Catholic Church exits: A) to fulfill God's mission – to preach the gospel to the world, B) to convert the world, and C) to provide a place for worship and administer the sacraments.

- Mass: Is the most important service to Catholics. It is a service of adoration and gratitude toward God in which Christ offers Himself through the ministry of the priest in a bloodless manner. Eucharist – the Lord's Supper – is a part of the Mass.

- *Seven Sacraments* (Sacrament literally means "sacred act"): There are two Categories – (A) "Sacraments of the dead" (which act as means of restoration - # 1 and # 2 below) and (B) "Sacraments of the living" (those that bring graces to the individual - # 3 through #7 below).

  1. Baptism: Removes original sin and actual sins. Baptism is done by immersion, sprinkling or by pouring water on the head. The water must touch the skin. Makes an indelible mark on the soul. In practice, baptism is usually performed on infant children of Catholic parents.

  2. Penance: For forgiveness of sins after baptism. Involving confession to the priest after examination of conscience. The priest absolves person of his sin and prescribes an act or actions of penance.

  3. Confirmation: The Holy Spirit coming to the baptized in a special way. Usually done after the baptized person has matured in age to be able to understand the doctrines of the Church. This sacrament makes an indelible mark on the soul.

  4. Eucharist: This is the part of the mass in which Christ is offered. Holy Communion is the person partaking of the sacrifice. As Christ is believed wholly present in either the unleavened bread or the wine, the communicant need only take one (usually the bread). It is believed that the bread and wine literally become the body and blood of Christ. Under special circumstances, the layman may partake of both kinds.

  5. Anointing of the Sick: Performed when in danger of death. Not only for healing but to restore a person to proper relationship with God. Anointed on eyelids, ears, nose, feet and forehead.

6. Holy Orders: Ordination to various ranks – Deacon, Priest, Bishop. The person ordained receives power and grace. An indelible mark is made on the soul.

7. Marriage: Only for some (not priests, monks or nuns). A baptized man and woman are bound for life and given grace or strength to live up to marriage standards.

- Seven Basic Precepts for Catholics:

    1. To Attend Mass on specified days, all Sundays and special holidays.

    2. Fasting: Those between ages 21 and 60 are bound as Catholics to follow Fast Days: Ash Wednesday and Good Friday. Fasting involves eating one full meal and two lighter ones with no in-between snacking, although liquids are allowed. Abstinence means going without meat and soup or sauces made from meat. Catholics aged 14-20 should abstain on Ash Wednesday and Good Friday. Friday abstinence for all is an obligation only during lent; however, Catholics are encouraged to make all Fridays special observances in honor of the Crucifixion.

    3. Confession or Penance: To examine self, repent to God and confess to a priest is expected at least once a year, usually before Easter.

    4. Easter Communion: To partake of sacrament of Eucharist during Easter time. Eucharist is to be kept at least once per year.

    5. Support of the Church: To financially support the Parish with its school, rectory, convent and church. Two general collections for the worldwide work are collected for Papal charities and for missionary work

    6. Observe Laws of Marriage: Church law requires two Catholics to be married before a priest and

two witnesses. It is sacramental if they are baptized Christians (non-Catholics) also. If non-Christians, it is still a *valid* marriage (provided no other impediments) but not sacramental.

7. To Help Spread Message: Responsibility of the lay members to spread Catholicism by example and evangelizing.

- Salvation: Heaven is for the saints. Purgatory is for those with stain of sin still upon them. Hell is for those who die with mortal sin. The hope of a Catholic is to experience the Beatific Vision. They will have fellowship with fellow saints in heaven. At death the soul goes to its assigned location (Particular Judgment). At the general resurrection, the body is united with the soul to enjoy the fullness of bliss with additional senses.

Purgatory is a place of purifying of the soul that will ultimately go to heaven. Prayers and the good works of loved ones on earth for the soul in purgatory will help shorten time spent there.

Hell is for the wicked that die with unrepented mortal sins. It is a place of torment and everlasting punishment in a fiery, bottomless pit.

SPECIAL BELIEFS:

- Transubstantiation – the belief that the bread and wine literally become the body and blood of Christ during the Eucharist

- Prayer to saints in heaven and purgatory

- Purgatory

- Limbus Infantium (a place of "natural happiness" where unbaptized babies go after death). This belief is no longer much discussed and is humorously referred to now being a doctrine that is "in limbo".

- Pope is the visible Head of the Church

- Veneration of relics

- Use of statues in worship

- Only true church

- Celibacy of Priests

- Great devotion to the Virgin Mary

- The church is the Kingdom of God on earth

- Apostolic succession

PROMINENT LOCATIONS:

Europe, South America, North America, Philippines. There is much growth of the Roman Catholic church in the developing world. World Headquarters is the Vatican City.

ORTHODOX CHRISTIANS

(c. 228 million adherents)

FOUNDER:

Jesus Christ in 33 A.D. Officially separated from Rome in 1054 A.D. over the procession of the Holy Spirit and the primacy of the Pope (Bishop of Rome).

GOD(S):

One God in the Trinity – Father, Son, and Holy Spirit who are Co-eternal. They maintain that God is a mystery whom man cannot comprehend.

SCRIPTURES:

Two sources of truth: The *Holy Bible* and Tradition. Orthodox Bibles contain the same books as in Protestant Bibles, they do not accept the extra books found in Catholic Bibles.

HISTORY:

When Christianity began, it was mainly located in the eastern part of the Roman Empire. It was in 313 A.D. that Constantine gave Christianity full equality with other religions in the Roman Empire. Constantine was baptized as a Christian shortly before he died. During the reign of Theodosius I (370-395 A.D.), Christianity became the official religion of the Empire.

There were five main centers of Christianity. They were: Jerusalem, Ephesus, Alexandria, Constantinople, and Rome. Only Rome was in the west. As a result, Rome often mediated in discussions and disagreements among the other four. Gradually Rome became dominant over

Constantinople. Rome took the liberty of adding the "filioque clause" to the Nicene Creed. This addition added the words "and the Son" to the Holy Spirit proceeding from the Father. This greatly disturbed the Eastern churches particularly the one at Constantinople. Over this issue and the primacy of the Bishop of Rome, the two groups split officially in 1054 A.D., excommunicating each other. The western became the Roman Catholic church and the eastern became the Eastern Orthodox church (Orthodox means "Right Belief"). They have remained separate ever since, although in 1964 the Patriarch of Constantinople and the Pope of Rome met and a year later cancelled the excommunications of each other.

Although there is still much separating them, both churches would like reconciliation under the proper conditions. The Eastern Orthodox Church remained imbedded in Eastern Europe, Russia and the Middle East while Rome expanded its influence throughout the world.

CHURCH ORGANIZATION:

The Orthodox are organized into ethnic groupings; for example: Greek Orthodox, Serbian Orthodox, Russian Orthodox, etc. They all look to the Patriarch of Constantinople as first among equals. Hierarchal form of government. They are not as strict as the Catholics in the governing of the churches.

CREED:

The official Creed is the Nicene Creed dating from 325 A.D. at the Council of Nicea.

BELIEFS AND CHARACTERISTICS:

- Liturgy: The prayers and ceremonies of their regular service. The priest performs the ceremony in which Christ is sacrificed. Concerning the bread and the wine (transubstantiation), their belief is similar to the Catholic belief.

- Sacraments: are similar to those of the Catholic Church with slightly different nomenclature:

    1. Baptism: Should be done as soon after birth as possible. Triple immersion is practiced.

    2. Chrismation: Is similar to Confirmation, but is done immediately after baptism. The baptized person is anointed with oil symbolizing the Holy Spirit.

    3. Eucharist: Partaking of the Bread and Wine. The leavened bread is placed in the wine and spoon-fed to the communicant. The priest and laity partake of both symbols.

    4. Penance: Sins are confessed and forgiven. The priest acts more like a counselor than a judge.

    5. Ordination: For a man becoming a Deacon, Priest, or Bishop. Priests may be married if married before ordination. Bishops may only be selected from those who are celibate.

    6. Marriage: The priest officiates in joining the couple in matrimony. The grace of God is expected to be bestowed upon the couple to help them fulfill this great commitment.

    7. Holy Unction: Anointing the sick. Usually for serious ailments, but not confined to life-threatening situations. The hope is for physical healing as well as comfort for the person – body and soul.

- Commandments: One should keep the Ten Commandments. (Historically, they especially stressed the commandment against making graven images in order to confound the Roman Catholics, but see "Icons" below.)

- The Church: as physical structures are laid out in the shape of a cross and decorated so as to give one the feeling of "heaven on earth." The church, as the body of believers, consists of those on earth, those in heaven (paradise), those in hell, and those recently deceased. They believe the church is One, Holy, Catholic, and Apostolic.

- Salvation: At death the soul goes to an intermediate state for a foretaste of what it will receive at the resurrection and judgment, either the joys of Paradise or the misery of Hell.

Christ will return at the end of time and judge the resurrected dead. The bodies will be reunited with the souls and be assigned to Paradise or Hell.

In Paradise will be peace, joy, fellowship with saints and angels, and the beatific vision of God.

Hell will bring association with demons, sorrow, and separation from God.

SPECIAL BELIEFS:

- Triple Immersion at Baptism.

- One true church. (Traditionally taught that the Roman Catholics separated from them.)

- Use of Icons – two-dimensional pictures, not three-dimensional statues. (Orthodox condemn statues as idols.)

- Have different dates for Christmas and Easter as they use the Julian calendar.

- Devotion to the Holy Spirit.

- Devotion to Mary (but not so much as in Roman Catholic practice).

- The Church is the Kingdom of Christ on earth.

- Belief in Apostolic Succession.

PROMINENT LOCATIONS:

Eastern Europe, Ethiopia, scattered communities in the Middle East and North America. Russia is the country with the greatest number of Orthodox Christians.

ANGLICANS / EPISCOPALIANS

(c. 77 million adherents)

FOUNDER:

Henry VIII is sometimes given credit as being the Founder, he was excommunicated from the Roman church in 1536, established the Church of England (Anglican church). Queen Elizabeth I (1559-1602), daughter of Henry VIII and Ann Boleyn, gave focus to the church. Episcopalians are the American version of the Church of England; they changed the name officially in 1784 after independence from Britain.

GOD(S):

Belief in the Trinity. God sharing Himself with mankind: the Father as Creator, the Son as Redeemer and the Holy Spirit as Sanctifier.

SCRIPTURES:

The *Holy Bible*, Tradition, and Reason are the three basic sources of their beliefs. They use the *Book of Common Prayer* for help and guidance in their worship.

HISTORY:

In the sixth century A.D., Augustine and several monks went to England and Christianity was planted in the British Isles. Nearly 1,000 years later Henry VIII was excommunicated by the Catholic Church after taking matters into his own hands regarding the dissolution of his first marriage in order to marry Ann Boleyn, hoping for a male heir to his throne. He decided to assume the role as head of the Church in England, and named his own archbishop. Henry maintained that any bishop had as much authority as the Bishop of Rome. Henry received his annulment from the Church of England. He then suppressed monasteries and put many Catholics to death. All the while Catholic doctrines were maintained.

Edward VI moved the Anglican church closer to Protestantism during his reign of six years (1547-1553). The first edition of *Book of Common Prayer* was produced during this time.

Queen Mary I tried to reverse the move toward Protestantism by reconciling with Rome (1553-1558). The effort was short-lived as Queen Elizabeth I soon re-established Anglicanism as the national religion in England. It was she who brought about the stability necessary to put the nation solidly in the Protestant camp. Reforms were made in doctrine and belief.

In 1784, after the American Revolution, William White led the way for the reorganization of the Church of England in America.

CHURCH ORGANIZATION:

The Archbishop of Canterbury is given top honor throughout Anglican-related bodies. However, each church is self-governing. Different countries generally have a governmental structure similar to the country in which it functions.

A democratic-type government prevails in the United States. A bishop presides over a diocese assisted by committees of laymen and priests. Several parishes make up a diocese. There are annual Diocesan and National Conventions with laymen and priests elected to attend for guidelines on their beliefs and various church programs. The Chief Bishop of the Episcopal Church presides at the national level.

There are three orders of the ministry: Bishops, Priests, and Deacons. Women may be ordained. Ministers may be married.

CREED:

Two are primarily used: The Apostles' Creed and the Nicene Creed.

BELIEFS AND CHARACTERISTICS:

- They are said to be Catholic in worship but Protestant in belief.

- They believe in two sacraments and five lesser rites:

  o The two main sacraments are: Baptism and Holy Eucharist. Baptism is usually infant baptism done by pouring water on the head (infusion) or by immersion. The Eucharist (or Lord's Supper) is kept in memorial of the sacrifice of Christ. Christ is believed present in it though not literally in flesh and blood. The Eucharist is the chief part of the Worship of the Church.

  o The five lesser rites are: Penance, Confirmation, Ordination, Matrimony, and Ministry of Healing.

- The Evolutionary Theory is held as the account of man's origin.

- Heaven and Hell are not believed to be literal physical locations but states of being.

- Church: There are two basic types of churches within Episcopalian circles: the "high" church, which has a rather elaborate service emphasizing the Catholic tradition. The "low" church service is much simpler with more of an emphasis on personal worship and the preaching of the gospel.

  Either church may be described as "broad" if it is liberal in its approach and is active in social programs.

  The church does not believe it is the only true church. All baptized Christians are considered members of Christ's body, although Episcopalians as well as Catholics and Orthodox believe they are "One, Holy, Catholic, Apostolic" churches.

- Salvation: Through Christ's sacrifice, they believe salvation means a new life lived according to God's Will. The final state of the dead will be decided at the judgment when God returns. Heaven for the saint and Hell for the sinner. In some of their literature they describe a paradise as a place for preparing the saint's soul for its final destiny.

Teaching regarding the Kingdom is fourfold:

- o Kingdom which is – The Church on earth.
- o Kingdom which is to come – The Church of the future.
- o Kingdom which was and is – The Church in heaven.
- o Kingdom which is within – Jesus in one's heart.

SPECIAL BELIEFS:

- A strong emphasis on the sacraments.

- Confession of sins before priest brings absolution.

- There are service orders such as monks and nuns.

- Belief in several creeds.

- Unbaptized infants won't go to hell when they die.

- They have no official stand on homosexuality.

- Nothing may be taught as necessary for salvation except it is proved by Scripture.

- Only bishops ordain.

PROMINENT LOCATIONS:

England, Canada, United States and tremendous growth in Africa.

LUTHERANS

(c. 48 million adherents)

FOUNDER:

Martin Luther (1483-1546) founded the Lutheran Church when he split with the Roman Catholic Church in 1517.

GOD(s):

Believe in the Trinity – Father, Son and Holy Spirit. One God in three persons.

SCRIPTURES:

The *Holy Bible* is their sole norm of belief.

HISTORY:

The son of a miner, Martin Luther had a rather strict upbringing. Though there were hard times, his family managed to send him to school. He decided to study law in the University of Erfurt. A near-death situation and a devout interest in religion led him to turn from law and enter a monastery. He was intelligent and vigorous in his religious studies. After two years, he was ordained a priest. In 1512, five years later, he received his doctorate. He began teaching at the University of Wittenberg.

Luther was bothered with thoughts of his sins and whether they were forgiven or not. He wondered whether the works attached to penance were essential for forgiveness. Nevertheless, he remained a professor-priest for five years. On a visit to Rome, he was unfavorably impressed with the pomp and riches of the priests there. He was particularly disturbed with the adoration accorded the Pope. Upon his return to

Germany, he tried to sort out his feelings. Then, he happened upon the words of Paul in Romans 1:17, "The just shall live by faith." These words deeply affected him.

As Luther was establishing his new line of thought (faith, not works, for forgiveness), a papal agent named Tetzel arrived in a nearby village to sell indulgences using such slogans as "with each coin that into my coffer rings / another soul from purgatory springs." An indulgence is the remission of the temporal punishment due to sins already forgiven, which the Church granted at that time in order to raise funds for the building of St Peter's Basilica in Rome. Luther spoke out against this practice of selling indulgences when members from his congregation in Wittenberg began subscribing to the practice.

On October 31, 1517, Luther posted 95 Theses on the church door at Wittenberg. This was the usual procedure for inviting discussion on a topic for debate. (See Appendix 10 for some of Luther's Theses). After nine months the Pope demanded Luther to appear at Rome. The meeting was changed to be at Augsburg at Luther's request. The meeting proved relatively fruitless for reconciliation. Luther continued to attack the actions of the Papacy until he was excommunicated in January 1521. He was to be treated as an outlaw by the church and many states. Northern Germany swung behind Luther as he had found favor with rulers in that region. Thus began the Protestant Reformation. Soon others followed the lead and became bold in their stance against Catholicism.

Luther married a former nun and fathered six children. Among his accomplishments were catechisms, hymns and his translation of the entire *Holy Bible* into German. Luther was known as strong and clear in his manner, but he has been criticized for being anti-Semitic and authoritarian in political beliefs. Luther died in 1546 after spending the last 16 years with chronic health problems.

His writings, catechisms and teachings still have quite an influence over the Lutheran Church. Lutherans became the largest worldwide body of Protestants.

CHURCH ORGANIZATION:

Early government of the Church placed it under the various princes. Later, a system similar to Episcopalians was followed. American Lutherans are largely congregational.

Three Main U.S. Church Groupings:

- o ELCA – Evangelical Lutheran Church of America now includes the Lutheran Church of America and the American Lutheran Church. These were the former liberal and moderate elements of Lutheranism.
- o Lutheran Church Missouri Synod – conservative
- o Wisconsin Evangelical Lutheran Synod – very strict

CREED:

The Augsburg Confession (1530)

BELIEFS AND CHARACTERISTICS:

- Justification by Faith and the Grace of God

- Priesthood of Believers (all believers have direct access to God)

- Two Sacraments – Baptism and Lord's Supper

- The *Holy Bible* is the sole norm of Faith

- Gospel about Christ and His work of forgiveness

- Sin is disobedience to God

- Obey God's will out of a grateful response to a loving Father

- Salvation: Is the gift of God, not of works. To live with Christ eternally. Baptism is required generally. Members should partake of Lord's Supper.

SPECIAL BELIEFS:

- Christ is present at celebration of Lord's Supper (Consubstantiation).

- Emphasis on faith, not works.

- Age 14 is the time for confirmation of youths.

- Five lesser sacraments are considered rites – confirmation, penance, anointing the sick, holy orders, and marriage.

- They believe they are the true religion. There are Christians in almost all other churches as well.

- Ministers may marry. Women may be ordained.

- A saint is a Christian.

PROMINENT LOCATIONS:

Northern Germany, the Scandinavian countries. In some countries it is the national religion. Many members in the United States.

PRESBYTERIANS

(c. 55 million including The Reformed Churches)

FOUNDER:

John Calvin (1509-1564), John Knox (1505-1572)

GOD(S):

One true God in three persons. The Father, of whom is the Son eternally begotten, and the Holy Spirit who proceeds eternally from both the Father and the Son.

SCRIPTURES:

The supreme source is the *Holy Bible*. Calvin rejected all practices not found in the *Holy Bible*.

HISTORY:

John Calvin was a distinguished student in his early formal education. He studied law and theology at the university level. He gained much training in Greek and Hebrew. After finding that one is saved entirely by grace, Calvin underwent a sudden conversion in his early 20's. He became quite austere in his religious beliefs. As a young reformer he was forced to flee his native France. He made Geneva, Switzerland his base. Calvin wrote and published his new understanding of religious beliefs. One famous work was *Institutes of Christian Religion*. He soon became one of the leading religious leaders of his time (he was 26 years younger than Luther). He agreed with the major reformation concepts such as: Priesthood of believers; Justification by faith alone, only two sacraments, and the *Holy Bible* as the only norm of faith.

After a few political/church skirmishes in Geneva, he became the most powerful person in the city in 1541. From Geneva, Calvin's version of Protestantism spread as disciples came from Holland, Scotland, England, and Germany.

John Knox established this faith in Scotland as the Church of Scotland. With the Puritans from England, Holland and Scotland, this faith was carried across the ocean to American soil. Believing in the need for a trained ministry led to slow growth in comparison with the Methodists and Baptists.

Presbyterians, Congregationalists, Dutch and German Reformed Churches all came from the Calvinistic brand of Protestantism.

The United Church of Canada is a mixture of Methodists, Presbyterians and Congregationalists. Many of the founding fathers of United States were Calvinist. Twelve of the fifty-five signatures of the Declaration of Independence belonged to Calvinist churches.

CHURCH ORGANIZATION:

Organized with elders in governing positions. Ordained ministers and elected laymen form the ruling group known as a "session." The session has supreme authority in spiritual matters of local churches. Presbyteries have rule over a certain area of congregations. Representatives of Presbyteries are organized into Synods.

The General Assembly is the highest court of appeals for Presbyterians.

The democratic process is used in electing governing officials. Laymen may hold the highest office of each court (Moderator).

Women as well as men may be ordained to the ministry.

CREED:

Westminster Confession of Faith. Also accepted are the Nicene and Apostles' Creed.

BELIEFS AND CHARACTERISTICS:

- Originally very strict in practice of beliefs.

- Depravity of man and the greatness of God are emphasized.

- Priesthood of all believers.

- Two Sacraments (Baptism and Lord's Supper).

- Justified by faith alone.

- The *Holy Bible* is the only infallible rule of faith and practice.

- Predestination – some men are chosen for heaven, others are not. Originally, double predestination was taught – some men are chosen for heaven and some are chosen for hell.

- Salvation is a gift of God. Good works are fruits of salvation. Heaven and hell are not only places, but also states of mind.

- Signs of the visible church:

  o Preach the pure gospel.
  o Observe the two sacraments.
  o Discipline sinners.

SPECIAL BELIEFS:

- Christ is spiritually received and nourishes partakers of the Lord's Supper. Grape juice and consecrated bread are received.

- At Confirmation, a person acknowledges what was done at his baptism. Laying on of hands is optional in some congregations.

- Even though there is a belief in the need for baptism, it is not essential to salvation. Faith is.

- May alter their confession of faith if necessary.

PROMINENT LOCATIONS:

Holland, Switzerland, Germany, Scotland, South Africa, South Korea and North America.

METHODISTS

(c. 50 - 75 million adherents)

FOUNDER:

John Wesley (1703-1791)

GOD(S):

Belief in a Trinity: God, the Creator Father; God, the Redeemer Son; God, the abiding Spirit.

SCRIPTURES:

The *Holy Bible* is their only authority. *Book of Discipline* is used for articles of faith.

HISTORY:

John Wesley was one of the few surviving of nineteen children born to Samuel Wesley, an Anglican priest, and his wife, Susanna. Susanna seems to have been more of the force in the family and was a strong influence in John's early life. At age 25, after his degree at Oxford and subsequent schooling, he was ordained an Anglican priest. John and his younger brother, Charles, founded a group bent on increasing its spirituality. They took communion weekly and studied in a disciplined manner. Because of their structured life, they acquired the name "Methodist". Their zeal for Bible study also earned them names such as "Bible Moths", "Holy Club" and "the Enthusiasts." Their original intent was not to start their own church. Their actions, however, set them apart sufficiently to make it essential that a new church be established. First as societies then as churches, Methodism entered the Protestant world. John Wesley took his methodical and strict manner to the American

Colonies in 1735, but his strictness of approach was not accepted. He met some Moravians on the ship to America and felt this led to a changed life and deeper conversion when he returned to Britain in 1737. Coming to the belief that he could ordain as well as Bishops, he took final steps in the 1780's to make separation from the Church of England complete.

Thomas Coke was appointed superintendent of the Methodist Churches in America later in the 1780's. (Missionaries had been sent in 1769.) Methodists in America were zealous to spread their faith to all. Circuit riders, such as Peter Cartwright, rode thousands of miles to reach new converts in far-flung locations to make Methodism the largest Protestant Church in America until 1920. Splits occurred over the slavery issue, but its broad appeal to all races thereafter made it the second largest Protestant fellowship in the USA. Since the 1970's, Methodist membership in the USA has declined strikingly as people have left to seek more conservative churches.

CHURCH ORGANIZATION:

The General Conference is the highest legislature body in the Methodist Church. It meets every four years. There are also executive and judicial branches. The executive branch is staffed by a council of Bishops elected by the ministry and laity. While democratic in model, parish ministers are appointed by the Bishop. There are numerous committees in the Church organization with laymen as well as ministers having prominent roles.

CREED:

Apostles' Creed – recited every Sunday.

BELIEFS AND CHARACTERISTICS:

- Traditional Protestant Theology with slight variations; similar to Anglican Theology.

- Baptism: For this "spiritual experience," sprinkling is the method commonly used. Babies may partake of it. It is called a ceremony for induction into the Kingdom.

- Lord's Supper: Observed as a memorial with bread and grape juice used as symbols of Christ's body and blood.

- Final Perfection: It is possible one may become perfect in this life. This teaching is one that originated with Methodists.

- Church and State: They believe in separation of Church and State.

- Liquor: Opposition to liquor has been a hallmark of Methodists. Fiery prohibitionist, Ms. Carry Nation and the Women's Christian Temperance Union were Methodist. The Prohibition Amendment to the US constitution was passed largely due to strong Methodist pressure.

- Social Activities: They are active in community social programs and strong in the ecumenical movement. There is wide latitude of beliefs from congregation to congregation.

- Salvation: Is by grace and involves life now lived according to the gospel. Heaven and hell concepts vary. Some believe they are literal while others believe they are merely states of mind or being.

- Sanctification: The Holy Spirit may produce a final perfection in us. They teach that God expects holiness in his servants.

- In recent years, Methodists have become more liberal and very tolerant.

- More American Indians follow this faith than any other church.

- One out of two Japanese American Christians belong to the Methodist faith.

PROMINENT LOCATIONS:

Mainly in United States and Canada.

BAPTISTS

(c. 100 million adherents)

FOUNDER:

John Smyth (1570-1611) is usually credited as Founder. Some say they go back to the days of John the Baptist.

GOD(S):

They believe in the Trinity – God manifested in Three Persons.

SCRIPTURES:

Baptists believe in the inspiration of the *Holy Bible*. Progressive and liberal Baptists do not consider some sections relevant for this time. Fundamentalist Baptists believe in its literal inspiration. There is no official teaching on how it may be interpreted though the scriptures are believed to be the final word on all doctrines.

HISTORY:

There are two lines of thought in this regard. One is called the secessionist view. That is the teaching of successive stages since the days of Christ. Tracing of their Baptist faith is linked to groups like the Waldensians, Paulicians, Albigensians, Catharists and Anabaptists who had ideas similar to the Baptists.

The second line of thought on their history stems from English Protestantism. John Smyth broke with the Anglican faith feeling they needed more purification. He fled to Holland with his followers in 1608. While there, he became acquainted with the Mennonites and Anabaptists (meaning re-baptizers). With their influence, he established the first Baptist Church in 1609. After John Smyth's death in 1611,

Thomas Helwys became the leading English Baptist and returned to England to organize the first Baptist Church on British soil. They preached the need for immersion baptism. Not finding freedom of religion in England, many Baptists emigrated to North America.

Roger Williams is credited with starting the first Baptist Church in Providence, Rhode Island in 1639. The Baptists spread their teaching rapidly in America. They became the first "convert" church in America, believing it was everyone's mission to spread the gospel. They were the first to forge west of the Mississippi with their preachers. Baptists became the largest religious group in the United States in the early 1800's. The Methodists overtook them in the 1820's, but over the years Baptists have grown to again surpass the Methodists (since 1920) and are the largest Protestant denomination in America.

CHURCH ORGANIZATION:

There are several large Conventions of Baptists. Southern Baptists are the largest group comprising some forty percent of all Baptists. They are conservative in thought and practice.

The National Baptist Convention and the National Baptist Convention of America (African-American groups) are the second and third largest, with nearly nine million combined. (In fact, nearly forty percent of all Christian African-Americans in the United States are Baptists.) The American Baptist Churches USA has approximately 1.4 million members and tends to be more liberal. There are numerous other smaller groupings in the Baptist tradition.

Each local church is autonomous and a law to itself. They operate on democratic principles where geographically possible. Any conventions merely give recommendations and help to promote missionary activity.

CREED:

No certain fixed creed to which all adhere.

BELIEFS AND CHARACTERISTICS:

- There is a wide diversity of beliefs owing to so much freedom of government for each local church. Yet, among the larger Protestant groups, Baptists would be the most conservative body.
- No sacraments – Lord's Supper and adult baptism by immersion are important *ordinances*. The Lord's Supper for believers only, and is generally taken once per month.
- Separation of Church and State.
- They look forward to the return of Christ to the earth.
- Hell is a reality – everlasting punishment of incorrigibles.
- Tend to be against all forms of worldliness – drinking, card playing, dancing, etc.
- Aside from the Seventh-Day Baptists, they keep a Sunday Sabbath.
- All are to be involved in spreading the gospel. Often have testimonies and experiences printed on leaflets and pass them out.

  o Women have been ordained as ministers.

  o "Once saved, always saved" view.

  o Bodily resurrection.

- Salvation involves:

  1. New Birth – Person becomes a new creature in Christ as a result of repentance, faith and baptism.

  2. Sanctification – Being set apart by God's Spirit.

  3. Glorification – The final happy state of the redeemed individual.

PROMINENT LOCATIONS:

United States, Africa, Asia, and England.

ANABAPTISTS: MENNONITES, AMISH AND THE BRETHREN

(c. 1.5 million in total: c. 1.1m Mennonites; c. 225,000 Amish; and c. 104,000 Brethren)

FOUNDERS:

Menno Simons (1496-1561), Jakob Amman (c. 1644- c. 1725)

GOD(S):

Traditional belief in the Trinity.

SCRIPTURES:

The *Holy Bible*. Follow the New Testament instructions strictly.

HISTORY:

The Anabaptist movement sprang from the Reformation; part of the movement in Switzerland was initially (c. 1525) called the Swiss Brethren. Menno Simons, a former Catholic priest, in 1536 joined a group in the Netherlands which stemmed from the Swiss Brethren. In 1693 Jakob Amman broke with the Swiss Brethren because they did not strictly enforce the rules of shunning (see below) causing a schism. At about this time, both the Swiss and Dutch/Northern German groups took their name from Menno; thereafter they were generally known as the Mennonites. At the same time, the group that followed Jakob Amman became known as the Amish. The Mennonites and Amish were persecuted in Europe and began to migrate to the American colonies from Germany and Switzerland in the late seventeenth century. Left alone in the new world they flourished. There are many splits and divisions within the Mennonite and Amish groups.

Church Organization:

Local congregations are autonomous. The ministry is made up of deacons, ministers and bishops. For the Amish, congregations are self-supporting. Brethren are organized with district and state conferences with elected delegates and General Assembly meetings are held every two years. Some Mennonite groups have state conferences.

Beliefs And Characteristics:

- Salvation is through repentance, conversion and baptism.

- There is a belief in future rewards and punishments.

- No oaths.

- No bearing arms or serving in the military (conscientious objectors). Exception: some Mennonite groups have been more recently willing to serve in the armed forces, and some serve in noncombatant roles in the military services.

- For the Amish, the Lord's Supper is celebrated twice each year with foot washing accompanying it.

Special Beliefs:

- To outsiders the primary distinguishing characteristic of the Mennonites is their rejection of the "world." They are against "worldliness." Depending on the group to which one belongs, varying amounts of modern dress, ways or technologies are permitted. Thus, the Amish use only horse and buggy for transportation and work on farms or in agricultural related employment (although many are also carpenters and craftsmen), while some Mennonites will drive cars only if the bumpers and all chrome parts are painted black so as not to be "prideful."

- German dialects are commonly spoken in the home and community of the Amish and many Mennonites. Their way of life is that of rural Germans as well. Anabaptists have carried over many European traditions from previous centuries.

- The practice of "shunning" or "meidung" is still practiced by the Amish and some Mennonites. Menno Simons taught that if a member had sinned or broke rules of the church, he would be expelled or excommunicated. If the excommunicated person does not repent, others in the community should have anything to do with him or her. Repentant members are always welcomed back.

- The ideal of success for the Mennonite is for children to join the church, carry on the farm, and raise up the next generation.

- As all Anabaptists ("re-baptizers"), they believe a person must be old enough to understand in order to be baptized.

- The Brethren, commonly known as "Dunkers" or "Dunkards," believe in baptism by immersion.

- In some groups, the men grow beards after marriage. However, moustaches and brass buttons on clothing are considered military and are not worn.

- The plain people (those who dress in traditional garb) dress as modestly as possible. Depending on their group, this could include women wearing bonnets in public, avoidance of bright colored clothing, and so forth.

- Amish church services are conducted in private homes by leaders who serve for life with no compensation.

- Barn raising is the most famous expression of community support. When a new barn needs to be constructed, all the members of the local community get together and build a new one in a flurry of activity. Within a day the new barn is raised.

PROMINENT LOCATIONS:

Mainly found in the United States (particularly in Pennsylvania, Ohio and Indiana), and Canada (particularly in Ontario and Manitoba). Many can also be found in Belize, Paraguay, Russia and the Democratic Republic of Congo (formerly Zaire). Interestingly, as a result of missionary activity, there are currently more Mennonites in Africa than in North America.

SOCIETY OF FRIENDS
(QUAKERS)

(c. 368,000 adherents)

FOUNDER:

George Fox (1624-1691)

GOD(S):

God is what one experiences and follows. No Trinity is mentioned. Jesus' teachings are valid, but there is no decisive teaching on His being God.

SCRIPTURES:

The truth comes from the *Holy Bible* and one's own Inner Light.

HISTORY:

As a young man, George Fox became dissatisfied with the Church of England. He left home and became a "Seeker" wandering about England looking for religious enlightenment. He desired direct access to God and believed he had found it when he heard a voice. He traveled the world preaching his particular beliefs. He and his followers were persecuted because of their pacifistic and unorthodox religious beliefs. They call themselves "Friends" but are called "Quakers" by others because at one time they were said to have "quaked at" or had a fear of God's Word.

In 1671, Fox visited the American colonies. Ten years later William Penn, a Quaker, founded Philadelphia, Pennsylvania, which soon became the leading city of the colonies. Quakers have always been very influential in America in spite of their small numbers.

Some famous Quakers: Susan B. Anthony, Paul Douglass, Herbert Hoover, and Richard M. Nixon.

CHURCH ORGANIZATION:

They have monthly, quarterly and yearly meetings to discuss business matters. Consensus of opinion and democratic procedures are used.

There are two types of services:

1. *Unprogrammed*
   Where Friends sit silently and wait to be moved to stand and speak. This is the more conservative form of worship.

2. *Programmed*
   Which involves preaching and music. This would be used in the more liberal groups.

BELIEFS AND CHARACTERISTICS:

- No formal creed.

- "That of God" is in every human being.

- Inner Light – Man has light in himself; God can inspire man by activating that light. The Divine Light of Christ is in every human.

- Man is basically good.

- No salaried clergy.

- Not Protestant or Catholic, but another way of life.

- No predestination.

- Heaven and hell are matters for private interpretation and beliefs.

SPECIAL BELIEFS:

- Denial of the Trinity.

- No Communion.

- No water baptism. It is a spiritual experience only.

- Plain folk image. They wear plain clothes and talk plain language such as "thee" and "thou." This characteristic is more prevalent in Conservatives.

- Pacifists: they do not serve in the military.

PROMINENT LOCATIONS:

The United States has over sixty percent of the total membership.

SEVENTH DAY ADVENTISTS

(c. 15.5 million adherents)

FOUNDERS:

1. William Miller (1782-1849)
2. Joseph Bates (1792-1872)
3. Hiram Edson (1806-1882)
4. Ellen G. White (1827-1915)

GOD(S):

Composed of the Father, Son and Holy Spirit – the Trinity.

SCRIPTURES:

The *Holy Bible* as interpreted by the writings of Ellen G. White. (The official Adventist teaching is that Mrs. White's writings are not scripture, but that Mrs. White had the gift of prophecy to interpret the *Holy Bible*.)

HISTORY:

Around 1824, William Miller, a Deist, through personal study of Daniel 8:14 became convinced that Christ would be returning 2,300 years after 457 B.C. (the date he believed Ezra led the return of the Jews to Israel). He believed Christ would return between March 21,1843 and March 21,1844. In 1833, Miller felt compelled to begin preaching about the imminent return of Christ or the Advent. At first his followers remained in their separate churches, but they soon began to form their own religious societies. This was the beginning of the Adventist Movement. Among those hoping for the imminent advent of Christ were some Sabbatarians, although they were a small minority. When nothing happened after March 21, 1844, William Miller and his followers sought to find the reason why. They interpreted Habakkuk 2:3 to mean that the advent would be in October. So, on October 9, 1844, William Miller proclaimed that Christ would return on the 22nd of October. Thousands prepared for the expected event. Some sold all they had. On October 22, 1844, thousands waited and watched for the return of Christ. Nothing happened. This day became known as "The Great Disappointment." The Millerites disbanded. William Miller admitted his mistake and had no further theories regarding the fulfillment of his prophecy of 1844. He died in obscurity in 1849.

One of the followers of Miller, Hiram Edson, could not believe they were in error and developed the doctrine of Investigative Judgment.

Another former Millerite, Joseph Bates, emerged as a leader in the Adventist Movement. He was a naval captain who believed in the Biblical dietary laws of clean and unclean meats, in abstinence, in vegetarianism, and in the seventh-day Sabbath. In 1846 (the year after the Seventh Day Adventist Movement was formed), he published a booklet on the Sabbath.

Ellen C. Harmon (White) was a young woman at the time of the "Great Disappointment." As a young girl, she had her nose severely broken and suffered from poor health all her life. She was raised in the Methodist Church but had joined the Adventists. She experienced her first vision at the age of 17. From that point on she was said to have been instructed by heavenly messengers from God. She was a prolific writer with over 50 books and 4,500 articles to her credit. She is respected by Seventh Day Adventists as possessing the gift of prophecy and of being able to clarify God's revelation to man. She married James White, an Adventist preacher, in 1846.

In 1846, Edson, Bates and White with their followers formed the Seventh Day Adventist Church (officially incorporated in 1860). It is the largest group of the Adventist Churches. Ellen G. White came to be the most prominent figure in the Church and led it until her death in 1915. The Church has continued to grow since her death. It has been claimed that the Church gains three members for each one it loses. Members are actively involved in the Church.

Church Organization:

Representative form of government. Lay members and ministers serve as elected officers. Ministers are usually graduates of Seventh Day Adventist colleges and have two or more years field experience. They have one of the largest parochial school systems in the United States.

Beliefs And Characteristics:

- Only true Church belief, but all people who love Christ will have some type of a chance.

- Original sin at fall of Adam.

- Trinity.

- Believers are baptized by immersion.

- Lord's Supper is kept four times per year with bread and grape juice.

- Belief in creation not evolution.

- Tithing system to support the Church.

- Very active in reaching out and helping others. Support schools and hospitals throughout the world.

- Use pictures of Christ.

- Unofficial women pastors.

Special Beliefs:

- Soon coming return of Christ (the Second Advent). Christ is to take His people to heaven for a thousand years while the earth lies desolate and empty (Isaiah 24:1, 3, 5-6). During the millennium, the earth will be the habitation of Satan alone. The saints will be in heaven judging the deeds of the wicked. All of the wicked will be destroyed by Christ at His coming and will await the second resurrection to receive their judgement.

- Investigative Judgment – On October 22, 1844, Christ went into the Holy of Holies in the heavenly temple to go over the books and determine who was righteous.

- Seventh Day Sabbath is kept from Friday sunset until Saturday sunset. Exceptions are made for helping others in hospitals and like circumstances.

- Observance of the clean and unclean meat laws although many avoid meat altogether and opt for vegetarianism.

- The soul sleeps at death until resurrection.

- Use Ellen G. White's interpretations of the *Holy Bible* to guide their understanding as she is believed to have had the "spirit of prophecy."

- There have been some claims regarding possible plagiarism by Mrs. White. The Church response was that a prophet's (or prophetess') thoughts can be inspired of God even if they are not original.

- Do not drink alcohol, coffee or tea.

- No smoking.

- Will serve in the military but only in noncombatant capacity.

PROMINENT LOCATIONS:

Although the denomination started in the United States, they now operate in nearly all countries of the world. Only 10% of church members currently live in the United States.

CHURCH OF JESUS CHRIST OF
THE LATTER DAY SAINTS

(Commonly called "Mormons")
(c. 13 million adherents)

FOUNDER:

Joseph Smith (1805-1844)

GOD(S):

God the Father, Christ (both made of flesh and bone), and the Holy Spirit (made of spirit). Man is to become God.

SCRIPTURES:

The *Holy Bible*, *The Book Of Mormon*, *The Pearl Of Great Price* and *Doctrines And Covenants* (which is still being added to as new revelations are received).

HISTORY:

In 1820, near Palmyra, New York, 14-year-old Joseph Smith, an unschooled member of a transient family, claimed to have witnessed the manifestation of the Father and Son in the woods near his home after praying for wisdom. Mormons believe Jesus Christ declared to him the need to restore the Christian Church as it had once been. Later, Joseph Smith and Oliver Cowdery, a believer friend, claimed Peter, James and John the Baptist ordained them. Smith was directed to find a set of gold plates inscribed with *The Book Of Mormon* in "Reformed Egyptian" and a set of crystal stone ("Urim and Thummin") with which to translate the plates. Although the plates were never seen by anyone else with anything other than "the eye of faith," eleven men swore to their existence. Before the plates and stones were taken back to heaven, Smith dictated *The Book Of Mormon* to others to record.

By June 1829, the book was finished and was soon thereafter published. On April 6, 1830 the "restored church" was organized in Fayette, New York. Both membership and hostility to the new church grew rapidly. The church was driven to Ohio, then Missouri, and then Illinois. There on the banks of the Mississippi they built the city of Nauvoo. In 1844, Joseph Smith was killed by a mob. Soon thereafter Brigham Young, abandoning Nauvoo, led the church to the Great Salt Lake Valley (1847). Because of their belief in polygamy, the U.S. Government refused to recognize Utah as a state until the practice was stopped. In 1890 when the church president proscribed polygamy, statehood was granted.

The schismatic Reorganized Church of the Latter Day Saints broke off from the main body of Mormons, in 1844, believing that Joseph Smith's descendants should lead the church and not Brigham Young.

CHURCH ORGANIZATION:

They believe they have the same organization as the early Christian Church. Over one half of each local group (called a "Ward") hold active positions in the Church. They include two priesthoods – Aaronic: with offices such as deacon, teacher, and priest; and the Melchizedek: with offices such as elder, the seventy, high priests, patriarchs, and apostles.

There are three layers of organization.

- The Ward – the local organization of churches.

- The Regional (stake) – composed of several Wards.

- The General – for the overall affairs of the entire Church.

Most in the organization are not salaried by the Church.

BELIEFS AND CHARACTERISTICS:

- Only true church

- Punished for your own sins not Adam's

- Conversion: repentance, faith, baptism, receive spirit

- Trinity is not a three-in-one God, but three separate personages

- Three-fold mission of the Church:

    1. To perfect the saints
    2. To preach the message of the restored gospel to the world
    3. To redeem the kindred dead

- The missionary work is carried out by all. Young men 19 and older are especially expected to serve two years at their own expense. Young women over 21 may serve for 18 months and older married couples serve for 6 - 18 months.

- Pictures of Christ

- Universal salvation

- Tithing

SPECIAL BELIEFS:

- At the time of Zedekiah, a group of Jews left Jerusalem and sailed to the new world. Here they separated into two groups: the fair skinned Nephites (who were righteous) and the dark skinned Lamanites (who were evil and whose descendants are the American Indians). In 33 A.D., the resurrected Christ appeared to these peoples in the Americas, and they became Christians. However, after a few decades the struggles began again, and by 384 A.D., the Lamanites annihilated the Nephites. Mormon, the Nephites' last general, gave the gold plates to his son Moroni who hid them. In 1829 Moroni, who had become an angel, showed Joseph Smith the plates.

- What God once was, man is; and, what God is, man will be."

- All people are spirits that have come to earth to live as mortals without memory of former existence – before going back to heaven as God's spirit children again.

- There will be a resurrection of the body to join the spirit that makes a soul.

- Temples – "Not secret but sacred" – only Mormons in good standing may enter. Non-Mormons may enter only when first built, prior to dedication. Uses:

    1. Proxy Baptism – Baptism for the dead (see below)
    2. Marriage for Time and Eternity (see below)
    3. Endowment – Rituals enacting "God's Plan of Salvation"

- Baptism for the Dead – To enter into glory all spirits must receive baptism, either while on earth or by another person on earth being baptized on their behalf.

- Marriage for Time and Eternity – In which it is believed the wife and children will be forever under their human husband and father in the life to come.

- Millennium is to be spent with Christ on earth. Christ will return to Independence, Missouri.

- Israel will be re-gathered in the Millennium.

- Lord's Supper is every Sunday with bread and water.

- Oaths are used in their temple service.

- Mary is God the Father's wife in heaven.

- Some Mormon sects still practice polygamy, however, the church officially teaches its members monogamy.

The smaller organization, The Reorganized Church Of Jesus Christ of the Latter Day Saints *differs* in the following areas from the larger Church of Jesus Christ of the Latter Day Saints:

- They reject polygamy.

- Different view about celestial marriage.

- Dissimilar regarding baptism for the dead.

- Have no temples or secret services.

- Believe God was always God.

- Christ was conceived by the Father as the only begotten of him.

The Reorganized Church Of Jesus Christ Of The Latter Day Saints is *similar* in the following areas:

- *Book Of Mormon*

- Restored Church belief

- Requirements are the same

- Both believe that Independence, Missouri, will be the Zion and is the site of the Garden of Eden.

PROMINENT LOCATIONS:

The Church of Jesus Christ of the Latter Day Saints has Salt Lake City and the state of Utah as its area of greatest density. Over half of all Mormons live outside of the United States, though. The Reorganized Church is centered around Independence, Missouri.

CHURCH OF CHRIST SCIENTIST
CHRISTIAN SCIENCE

(c. 300,000 adherents)
Estimates only, as membership statistics are prohibited.

FOUNDER:

Mary Baker Eddy (1821-1910)

GOD(S):

Variously referred to as great mind, father-mother God, Spirit, Soul, Principle, Life, Truth, Love, and a Trinity, Three offices of one divine principle.

SCRIPTURES:

The *Holy Bible* and *Science And Health With Key To The Scriptures* by Mary Baker Eddy.

HISTORY:

Mary Baker Eddy is the only woman in history to have solely founded a religion. Raised in New England, her childhood was marred by continual illnesses. Well-educated and emotionally sensitive, she believed she heard the voice of God at age 8. She was interested in philosophy, logic and moral science, and her religious beliefs reflect this. She was first married at age 22, but her husband died the next year. This was a traumatic event in her life. She later married a dentist, but this marriage ended in divorce in 1873. She married Asa G. Eddy in 1877 who died five years later. Seeking relief from her physical problems, she sought the help of a faith healer named Phineas P. Quimby whose ideas of "animal magnetism" and "metaphysical healing" appeared later as part of her religious beliefs.

In February of 1866, she slipped on ice in Lynn, Massachusetts. While recovering she read Matthew 9:2-8 and from this point the "truth of healing" was understood by her and she was "in better health." Teaching that all disease was mental, she went on in 1876 to found the Christian Science Association. In 1879, the Mother Church at Boston was founded and Christian Science as we know it officially began. *The Christian Science Monitor*, which began in 1908, continues to be a very reputable newspaper.

CHURCH ORGANIZATION:

Practitioners, approved by the Mother Church, pray for the sick that ask for prayers on their behalf. Two readers elected every three years by the local members to read from the *Holy Bible* and *Science And Health* at church services.

They have only one church, the Mother Church, in Boston, Massachusetts; and all 3,200 other chapters are branches of the Mother Church.

BELIEFS AND CHARACTERISTICS:

- Only the spiritual is real, the physical is unreal. God is Spirit and everything real is a reflection of Him. God is "all-in-all." Nothing possesses reality or existence except as divine mind or ideas.

- Baptism is "a continual happening."

- Communion – Sit quietly at church twice yearly.

- All causation is mind, all effect is physical.

- There are women as well as men practitioners.

- Salvation is to be saved from your illusions.

- Sin is belief in life apart from God.

- Heaven and hell are present states of thought.

- In reality you have good health – you just don't have your mind on God.

- Jesus was a human being; Christ was the divine idea.

- Evil doesn't exist because God is God and He is all; therefore, evil is another illusion.

- Illness is an illusion to be dispelled by God. Healing is emphasized because it is believed to be the primary indication that man must go back to God.

- They generally reject medical treatment, as illness is an illusion – but will go to doctors to set bones and deliver babies.

PROMINENT LOCATIONS:

Mainly in the United States – but has influence worldwide.

SALVATION ARMY

(over 2 million adherents)

FOUNDER:

William Booth (1829-1912)

GOD(s):

The Trinity

SCRIPTURES:

Believe in the inspiration and authority of the *Holy Bible*

HISTORY:

William Booth was a Methodist minister in London who concentrated his efforts to reaching out to the underprivileged. Because of differences in emphasis, Booth felt obliged to break away and form his own group, which was called the East London Christian Mission or the Hallelujah Army. In 1878 it became known by its present name, Salvation Army. The Salvation Army set up congregations in the United States by 1880 and in Canada by 1882. Their enthusiasm and zeal to serve others, both physically and spiritually, has contributed to their growth. It is estimated that there are today some 17,000 officers, over 1 million soldiers, and millions of volunteers. Because of their outstanding involvement with the underprivileged and needy, they have the best record for finding missing persons even surpassing law enforcement agencies.

CHURCH ORGANIZATION:

Booth modeled the organization after the British Army. The ministry is referred to as officers; their churches are called citadels; and their missions are referred to as corps. Ranks of the officers are similar to those of the British Army. An officer must wear his uniform at all times and may only marry another officer.

BELIEFS AND CHARACTERISTICS:

- Man, through repentance, faith and "regeneration" can be saved. But, he can fall away if he neglects proper holy living.

- Fall of man

- Immortal Soul

- Heaven and Hell

- Resurrection of the body

- Beliefs similar to Methodism

- No Predestination

- No tobacco, gambling, or liquor

- Music plays an important role in their services

- General judgment at the end

- Equal rights for women

- They use military-sounding terminology (For example: "Knee drills" is used in reference to prayers.)

SPECIAL BELIEFS:

- The mission of the Church is the spiritual regeneration of mankind. Physical works are done to help reach people spiritually.

- No nominal members are allowed. Must become a "soldier" if belong to the Church.

- No Baptism

- No Communion

PROMINENT LOCATIONS:

Are in over 110 countries worldwide with International Headquarters in London, England. A large contingent and work is conducted in the United States, and they are very active in refugee camps in Africa.

JEHOVAH'S WITNESSES

(over 6 million actively involved members)

FOUNDER:

Charles Taze Russell was the original Founder (1852-1916). Upon his death in 1916, "Judge" Joseph Rutherford became the Church's leader and greatly altered the Church's teachings.

GOD(S):

Jehovah God. The Holy Spirit is not a person but an active force. Jesus Christ is the Archangel Michael and is not God, but is referred to in their *New World Translation of the Holy Bible* as "a god" (Hebrews 1:8 and John 1:1).

SCRIPTURES:

The *Holy Bible*. Their own translation, *The New World Translation*, is widely used.

HISTORY:

Charles Taze Russell, a Pittsburgh, Pennsylvania, businessman, was disturbed by the doctrine of hell. He developed an interest in biblical chronology and predicted Christ would return in 1874 to the earth and that in 1914 Armageddon would begin. In 1879, Russell began to publish the magazine *Zion's Watchtower* (now known as *The Watchtower*, with over two million copies sold in 200 countries). In 1884, he legally incorporated the "Zion's Watch-tower Bible and Tract Society." Later, he came to believe that 1914 was the year that the Messianic Kingdom was established in heaven and that Christ had returned secretly. His wife divorced him after this, and he was accused of selling a fake cancer cure, "millennial beans" and "miracle wheat." Russell was zealous for his beliefs – preaching some 30,000 sermons and writing some 50,000 pages of material.

After Russell's death in 1916, Judge Joseph Rutherford (1869-1942), Russell's attorney, assumed the leadership of the Church until his death. While Russell lived, Rutherford spoke highly of him, but soon after his death, the "Judge" began to remove many of Russell's original teachings (such as: "The Great Pyramid" and some prophetic pronouncements). He also sought to destroy the personality cult that had been established around Russell. Rutherford introduced the concept of "Jehovah" and of "God's Sovereignty." The United States government accused the Witnesses of being German agents and imprisoned the Church leaders. Rutherford stressed pacifism, witness work, and not saluting the flag or voting. Church membership shrunk because of persecution.

In 1942, Nathan Knorr became the new leader, serving in that capacity until his death in 1979. Under his leadership, the more extreme aspects of the Jehovah's Witnesses' beliefs and behaviors were modified.

CHURCH ORGANIZATION:

A non-incorporated body, the Jehovah's Witnesses (name adopted in 1931) uses the nonprofit Watchtower Bible and Tract Society to do their witnessing. All members are considered ministers. No man is appointed as head of the congregation. A body of ten ministers oversees the preaching and teaching activities. All the workers in the field and at the Brooklyn, New York Headquarters are volunteers. Workers and officers in Brooklyn receive room and board plus a small financial compensation. Women may not preside over a congregation of men and teach them, although they are ministers also.

BELIEFS AND CHARACTERISTICS:

- Belief that they are the one true faith.

- Go to church on Sunday even though they believe every day is the Sabbath.

- No observance of Christmas, Easter or other holidays of this world.

- The soul sleeps at death, awaiting the resurrection.

- No voting

- No tobacco

- No titles for the ministry

- No gambling

- Drunkenness is condemned

- No flag saluting

- Baptism is by complete immersion as a sign of submission to Jehovah and this makes a person a minister.

SPECIAL BELIEFS:

- The millennium will be on the earth. This will be a time of the vindication of Jehovah's name and of a thousand-year reign by Christ.

- Christ has been invisibly present since 1914 on the earth.

- Passover is kept yearly on the 14th of Nisan. However, the symbols of bread and wine may only be taken by those few of the 144,000 who are still alive.

- Only the first 144,000 Jehovah's Witnesses go to heaven as spirits at the end, all others will live forever on the earth as resurrected flesh and blood human beings.

- No blood transfusions as they consider this to be a violation of the scripture against eating blood.

- Hell is the grave.

- They are conscientious objectors.

- Jesus Christ was the first created being.

- Witnesses believe all members should be actively spreading the Word. They draw up plans to canvas every inhabited area in the countries they have reached. The typical member averages some 11 hours per month of missionary work in his or her area.

- The "Times of the Gentiles" are 607 B.C. to 1914 A.D.

PROMINENT LOCATIONS:

Worldwide influence with a heavy concentration in the United States.

PENTECOSTALS / CHARISMATICS

(c. 520 million adherents of Pentecostal churches or are Charismatic within their own church - note: many of these are also included in the numbers of denominations covered previously)

FOUNDER:

Charles Parham (1873-1929)

GOD(s):

Trinity

SCRIPTURES:

Primarily the New Testament

HISTORY:

Charles Parham, a Methodist minister in the holiness tradition, asked his Topeka, Kansas, Bible class to search the *Holy Bible* for any evidence of the baptism of the spirit. They came to believe that Glossolalia, speaking in tongues, was the only evidence of a "second baptism". During a revival meeting on January 1, 1901, Agnes Ozman, one of his pupils, became the first person to "speak in tongues." Thus the Pentecostal movement began. In 1906, the black ghetto of Los Angeles, California, became the center of the movement with the establishment of the Azusa Mission. Today, it is estimated that almost 10% of the world's population attend Pentecostal churches or are charismatic members of major church denominations. Pentecostal churches are among the fastest growing churches in the world.

CHURCH ORGANIZATION:

Speaking in Tongues (Glossolalia) is a movement within various churches and not a single church.

BELIEFS AND CHARACTERISTICS:

- Every Christian can expect a "second baptism." This conversion is proved by speaking in tongues, which are not human languages. Glossolalia is considered a modern day revival of the primitive church.

- Interpreters are present in services to translate the tongues into the vernacular.

- The "tongues" spoken usually have no similarity to any known language. Linguists have found no correlation between the "tongue" and the subsequent "interpretation" in analytical studies.

- Lively, loud, spontaneous, disorganized church services with some making sounds beyond their normal human speech patterns. Trance-like states of disassociation are created.

- Strict Fundamentalist Protestant beliefs frequently held in common:

  o Only believers are baptized (by immersion)
  o Women do not wear makeup
  o *Holy Bible* is inspired Word of God
  o No tobacco
  o Sunday is their day of worship
  o Heaven and hell
  o Immortal soul

PROMINENT LOCATIONS:

Worldwide it is estimated that there are 130+ million members of Pentecostal churches and an additional 390+ million people of various churches who consider themselves Charismatic. Pentecostals and

Charismatics are found in almost every nation on earth. They have especially grown rapidly in the developing world.

APPENDICES

Appendix 1

Magic, Religion and Man

There is a continuum between basic religion, magic and science that raises some interesting psychological and cultural issues. In this appendix we will examine specifically the first two parts of the continuum, magic and religion, paying special attention to the area of (what we would term) magic (or superstition) as it relates to various cultures. Science and Technology will also be briefly touched upon as it relates to magic.

In magic a person or supernatural being was thought to be able to force nature to do what that person willed, something which nature would not normally do. As time passed, however, technology replaced this view (because technology actually worked) with a slightly different philosophic approach: a person doesn't have to force nature to do something unnatural, instead humans could exploit a natural (but perhaps undetected) harmony within nature. The scientist of today is less like the magician of mythology that forced nature to do the unnatural and more like the elves or dryads of mythology that worked with nature to encourage it to do what it had the potential of doing. Men do not break the laws of nature by using technology, but exploit them. By the time that Francis Bacon was writing the transition was complete: "Knowledge is power...We cannot command nature except by obeying her." Yet it is within this exploitation that danger lurks. It has just been in the past hundred years that people have begun to realize this in seeing the effects that our science has had on the environment of our planet. For example, because of medical science people live longer, but this has the side effect of having more people to be fed and more land needing to be developed/deforested, and so on.

2 Views of the World

One of the most outstanding features of humans in the Modern Age – particularly those who are more highly educated in the western manner – is that people today, as compared to the past, are unaware or unwilling to be aware of any unseen world. This is largely as a result of the triumph of science and technology in education and in the obvious physical comforts and helps that it has bestowed upon people. However, this western view of reality for most people still includes some generally recognized aspects of the unseen world in the area of the religious. Thus, in the west, there is a two-tiered system with science here, in our daily lives, and religion seen as something above (or as a primitive hold-over from a superstitious past) that is generally disregarded in daily life by most westerners.

Outside of the west, there remains another, alternative view. It could be considered a three-tiered view, with religion above, science or the physical world below, and a third area in the middle. This third, middle, area could be considered a sort of mesocosmos – a part of reality where the unseen world impinges on ordinary life. The Mesocosmos could be thought of as an area of popular or folk interpretations of strange (to a westerner) things that happen. It could be thought of as a sort of place in a theology of the "demonic".

These 2 views of reality could be represented as follows (Augsburger, p. 34):

Western 2-tiered View	Historic/Multicultural 3-tiered View
1. Religion Faith in God, the spiritual dimension, the sacred, miracles and exceptions to the natural order.	***1. High Religion*** *Cosmic beings*: God, gods, angels, demons, or a world separate from this one. *Cosmic forces*: Kismet, fate, karma, or impersonal cosmic forces.
(Excluded Middle)	***2. Low Religion, Magic, Mana***
	Folk religion: local gods and goddesses, ancestors, spirits, demons, ghosts. *Psychic phenomena*: curses, blessings, special powers, astrological forces, evil eye. *Physical phenomena*: magical rites, charms, amulets, fire walking, embedded charms, psychic surgery.
2. Science	***3. Natural and Social Science***
Sight and experience, the natural order, secular definition, empirical methodology, mechanical analogies, sense experience, experimentation and proof.	Directly observable sensory phenomena, knowledge based on experimentation and replication. Interaction of human beings or interaction of natural objects based on natural forces.

In the three-tiered view, there are aspects shared by most of the basic religions. When these are examined, it can be clearly seen that the three-tiered view, which includes magic, is helpful in understanding people's view of reality in the past (which included an awareness of the unseen world).

8 Common Features of Basic Religions

Hopfe gives eight common features of basic religions (p. 22-30). It is clear that some elements of basic religion are still kept in modern, technological cultures, thus highlighting the perceived value that people continue to derive from them:

1) *Animism* – nature and the world around is alive with spirits and mystical forces (personal or impersonal). Anima is Latin for Spirit; physical things such as rocks may also have anima. Mana is what impersonal force is called (sort of like a "spiritual electricity"). Animism usually results in a great reverence for nature, often out of fear or desire for help.

2) *Magic* – Attempting to force nature to one's will. (A) Homeopathic or imitative magic is when people ritually act out what they want to happen (could this be similar to certain visualization techniques?). (B) Contagious magic is when it is believed that any two things that were once associated maintain a mystic link with each other. (C) Sympathetic Magic attempts to coerce nature to behave in a certain manner by performing that act oneself on a smaller scale. Sticking pins in Voodoo Dolls would be an example of both B and C. (D) A Fetish is an object that controls nature in a magical fashion (example: lucky rabbit's foot). Magic, with its emphasis on getting the desire of the user of magic to have his/her will be done, stands slightly off from Religion (which could be described as the attempt to influence the gods to respond favorably to human requests) and Science (which could be described as working with nature to obtain the desired result). However, things are never this clear cut. In Vanuatu (formerly the New Hebrides) there is a religion called the John Frum Cargo Cult. During the second world war, stone-age natives were exposed to the tremendous influx of American technology and wealth. They perceived the technology as magic and went on to form a religion out of it.

3) *Divination* – Seeing into the future, usually through the use of the examination of a naturally random source (entrails, dice, tortoiseshell, etc) or by one who was possessed of the spirits, such as a shaman.

4) *Taboo* – Certain actions and objects must be avoided so as not to anger the spirit world. In some religious traditions people do not eat pork or shellfish, which may have originally come from a desire not to make God angry with us.

5) *Totems* – Some primitive religions express the kinship they feel with nature by identifying themselves with a particular animal. This is an extension of Animism. National symbols and symbols of athletic teams may come from this characteristic of basic religion.

6) *Sacrifice* – One of the most common practices of all religions. It is variously considered in terms of feeding the spirits, giving a gift to the spirits or establishing a bond between men and the spirits.

7) *Rites of Passage* – Certain rituals are carried out at key points in the life of a person (birth, puberty, marriage, and death being the most common). This is almost a universal human characteristic. After each rite of passage, additional knowledge, rights and responsibilities are often given.

8) *Worship of Ancestors* – believing that the departed person lives on after the death of the body (perhaps because of dreams or visions) led to efforts to avert the evil the dead might do. Ancestors are worshipped to also please the dead so that they will benefit the living.

WEST AFRICAN ANIMISM

At the university where we used to teach, there was a very large percentage of "international" (i.e. non-US) students. One of the African students had been the village chief in one of the animist tribes of Nigeria. We became friends and once gave a presentation about the religious/magical world that he grew up in. Much of what follows in the next three paragraphs comes from that presentation, a few other facts came from questions that we asked him later.

In West Africa, most tribes have always believed in a personal god. Christianity or Islam are outside religions which overlay the traditional beliefs still practiced by the people. The traditional "witch doctor" in a tribe represents god to the people. The native doctors function as priests/mediators. Every god has a shrine. Every shrine has an attendant. How does one get to be a high priest? He starts acting strange, predicting the future, etc. The Medicine man/native doctor can contact any god (unlike priests who can only contact their specific god). They are good with herbs to make remedies. Since they are trying to work with nature their remedies often work.

There is Ancestor worship in which the spirits of those dead return to reside and protect the family. The heads of households when they die are usually buried under the floor in their homes. Powerful men are often eaten rather than buried. In Africa when you are cursed by a god you become "osu" – outcast – and are sold into slavery. In marriage, reincarnation can only occur through women who are virgins when married. If a man discovers otherwise the marriage is annulled. In marriage, the ancestral gods can only come to the earth through women that are pure.

These things are real to these people. It is not that they are foolish or ignorant. For them the world is alive with unseen spirits. Worship is either: 1) of ancestors, 2) of the gods. Personal spirits ("chi") convey problems to the spirit in charge of the village (great god). There is a system of gods, but generally no access to the supreme god. The hierarchy of spirits looks like this:

1. Supreme god ——————
2. Intermediary gods ———
3. Ancestral gods ———
4. Personal spirits ———

West African village culture is thus intertwined with the animist approach to life. On a daily basis basic religion offers the people a structure for their lives. But basic religions and magic may also offer more complex insights into the way reality is.

CONCLUDING EXAMPLES

In our own experience, we have seen how belief in the unseen world is alive and well in the modern North America: and not just in the area of Religion, but perhaps even more so in the middle, or mesocosmos, section of the three-tiered understanding of reality. When I (Douglas) went to work for a company in New York city, the people that I worked with were all college educated, professional, and were dealing in a branch of financial services were we were actually making our livings by rigorous application of statistics applied to business. Before going there it had been my belief that gambling was a tax on people bad at math, yet here was a bunch of accountants, actuaries, etc. who gambled an inordinate amount and who were all convinced that there was such a thing as Luck. Here was an area of Superstition within the modern world (lucky numbers and gambling at an office full of educated people making their living off of probabilities!) existing side by side with the American culture's institutional belief in a view of reality that does not allow a world of the unseen to exist in quite this way.

What can be even more unexpected to us is the way atheists or agnostics can display understandings that can only be described as magical or mystical. Often, those who have a non-religious, "scientific" approach to life, can come forth with some ritualizing behaviors and beliefs. For instance, there is a part of every 12-step program to overcome addiction that involves God/god being involved and called upon to help in the healing of the person. People may also make decisions that are contrary to their economic or mental well-being based on superstition. For example, I (Douglas) have a friend in Israel who is an atheist, yet lives his life by the astrological charts. Some of those who have no use for religion, have still made room in their lives for magic!

Appendix 2

Chinese Folk Religion

Aside from the "Three Truths" (Taoism, Confucianism, and Buddhism) covered previously in the main text, there is also a particular folk religion of the Chinese people which should be kept in mind. It consists of the beliefs and practices of the great masses of the common people from about the end of the first millennium AD until the communist revolution in 1948. It was still privately practiced in many Chinese families since that time, and has experienced a recrudescence in the past few decades.

The English term "religion", in a Chinese context, is not completely clear. The Chinese word for religion is *Chiao*. It can refer both to an organized religion (like Islam or Roman Catholicism) and also to a philosophy of how to live life. In fact, in Chinese thought there is not much of a distinction made between religion and philosophy.

The Chinese could be considered as having an approach to religion different than in West Asia, Europe or the Americas. Some scholars refer to the Chinese as having "naturalistic" or "humanistic" religious views. For instance, the world is natural and what human beings are and do is natural. The world exists just as it is, and therefore it is pretty well as it is supposed to be. Unlike the world religions that began in the Middle East (Judaism, Christianity and Islam), which define religion as a belief and faith in God, the Chinese do not necessarily see it that way, especially if such a belief separates them from the realm of god(s). Middle Eastern religions look at God as supernatural, a being that is above and beyond nature, and they frequently consider this world sinful and to be rejected in preference to a better life to come. In Chinese thought there is no such division between God and the universe.

Chinese strive to make the maximum use of this world, by living in harmony with it. A person should try to find happiness both now and in the future, both on earth and in heaven (*T'ien*).

Doctrines and churches stressing a inflexible body of beliefs were rare in traditional China. In fact, most people would take from any religion whatever they felt was best. Chinese assumptions for how to live life and religion are as follows:

a) Life and the world are natural (not "fallen," but they are as they are supposed to be).
b) God(s) are not outside of the world.
c) People, spirits and gods (in each the material and the spiritual world) are in contact (they can communicate between worlds by dreams, etc.).
d) The nature that is in any thing (and which is good) can be encouraged to flower.

Ancestor Veneration – the oldest and most common expression of Chinese folk religion, also called "ancestor worship". It is founded on the belief that the dead, which dwell in a world of spirit, still constantly interacted with their descendants who were still living. Not only did the living and the dead communicate, but they also effected the fortune of the others on each side of death. For instance, a living person's bad behavior could damage their ancestors ghosts in the other realm. Because death does not do away with a person (they just go to the other world) the obligations of the living to their dead ancestors continue.

Chinese homes often had a shelf on which sat pieces of wood with the names, titles, birth and death dates of the dead ancestors. Family ceremonies occurred commonly on the first and fifteenth days of the (lunar) month, on birth and death dates and on some festivals. Ancestors were offered food (which the family later ate), were told of things that happened in the family, were bowed to and enjoyed candles and incense burned in their honor.

Souls – People have 2 souls (*shen*), one good and one bad. This belief changed over time and from place to place. A person had to take care of the souls of his/her ancestors, and the Emperor had to care for the souls of his subjects, particularly those without descendants. The soul was thought to be in the breath, the shadow or the heart. This is why breathing exercises are found in both Chinese medicine and exercise.

Fortune / Luck – Astrology and Horoscopes were very important to Chinese (with different symbols than are found in the West), and used frequently. *Feng Shui* ("Wind and Water") is a form of Geomancy – the study of land, building and weather forms to shape fate or tell fortunes – and is very important to this day. I (Douglas) know of companies in Asia that make Feng Shui a part of their businesses, even down to how their offices are laid out. It is believed that your personal or family's fortune is influenced by the layout and location of your home (for instance, a house on a hill that looks like a dragon's back would be considered a good site). Good things include: dragons, the south, trees, tigers, foxes, phoenixes, unicorns, cranes, trees, mirrors, books and flags.

Heaven – (called *T'ien* "Sky"), was very similar to the average Christian's image of heaven. It is ruled by the "Jade Emperor" or the "Old Man in Heaven" (old man being a term of respect in Chinese). Here there were gods, demons, spirits and ghosts, all organized into a heavenly society, with shifting duties and powers.

The Jade Emperor is the Chinese equivalent to the Supreme Being: omnipotent, just, good, a law giver, and a sustainer. Human rulers did these same things only at his mandate, which, if removed, it was believed that national calamities would occur. Of the lesser gods, the Kitchen god (god and goddess in the north) was the most important and had a place in every Chinese kitchen. Other notable gods included the Dragon King (god of rain) and *Ts'ai-Shen* (god of wealth), *Kwan-Yin* (patroness of mercy), *Yen-Lo Wang* (lord of death).

Demons – Evil spirits (*gwei* translated "devil" or "demon") cause of sickness and bad luck. They can be tricked (fooled to go away by statues of scary looking monsters, for example) and can only move in straight lines (hence bends in corridors to prevent their coming into homes or offices). Since they liked to cause problems for people who had good fortune, people would often not brag about what they had (for example not speaking too much of good things like their children) in order for demons not to take notice.

Spiritualism – At one time, all villages had a *Wu*, a shaman or medium who would allow himself to be possessed by spirits or ghosts.

Appendix 3

Caste System in Hinduism

One of the aspects of the Hindu religious system which is often considered merely cultural, but which was usually (but not always) given in source material as a primary belief, is the Caste System. This is often deemphasized in Hindu material and explanations designed for non-Indians, as being considered somewhat an embarrassment by the more democratic-minded or modern Indians. However, one university educated twenty-something friend of mine (Douglas) who is a Brahmin, was raised in the United States, eats hamburgers, etc., surprisingly told me recently that she feels that the caste system is important.

Within the Caste System all people are born into one of four levels or castes:

1. Brahmin – Holy men
2. Kshatriya – Rulers and warriors
3. Vaishyas – Merchants and craftsmen
4. Sudras – Commoners
   Below these are the casteless Untouchables (Dalits)

Each caste has its own specialized duties (Dharma). It is believed that your birth to a particular caste was due to Karma from your previous lives. About the most positive reference that we consulted on this subject accused people critical of the system as being "sociocentric" and not understanding the cultural value system underlying the castes: different castes receive returns proportional to the social value that they add to the community (Augsburger, 158). Indian social structure has proven to be remarkably stable over many centuries, which could be considered a good thing. In interviewing people who come from India, many today have a much more negative view of what the caste system does in stifling improvement and hope for a person's future. Taking the religious aspects of the caste system and comparing them with 20th century American beliefs regarding God, humans, animals, plants and inanimate objects respective places in the universe, we get the following:

American Concept of Life

God: Eternal, supernatural, infinite
(relations between God and man
are vertical)

Man:
Natural, but with an eternal soul.
A--------------B
Relations between men are
essentially horizontal.

Animals: temporal

Plants
Inanimate World: lifeless

Indian Concept of Life

Brahman: The only reality,
unknowable to the passing world

High gods
Lesser gods
Demons and spirits
Demigods
Saints and incarnations
Priests
Rulers
Merchants
Craftsman castes
Worker castes
Service castes
Outcastes

High animals
Low animals
Plants
Inanimate world

Creator ← →Creation

Pure Spirit ←------------- Mixed ------------→ Pure Matter

Reality ← →Illusion
←----Relations are all essentially vertical ----→

Appendix 4

Nirvana in Buddhism

The goal of all this in Buddhism is Nirvana, a blowing out or extinguishing of self and desire, a supreme bliss. Anyone can find salvation, regardless of caste. You just have to do your part. There is the idea of rebirth in Buddhism, but it is quite different (and a lot harder to understand) than in Hinduism. Because of Karma – the same law of cause and effect that comes from Hindu philosophy – a person is "the architect of his own fate" (Saddhatissa, 18). During the course of the present life a person has the free will to mold her own Karma, in fact it is "possible for anyone to obliterate most of his Karma through meditation" (Ibid., 18). Most may not in fact do this, but it sounds more encouraging and less difficult to do than the achievement of Moksha in Hinduism.

Regarding rebirth in Buddhist philosophy, the soul does not exist as consciousness (as it does in Platonic philosophy and Hindu Atman theory)– in fact personality doesn't exist forever – a person "is as it were reborn every moment" since the mind and body are continually changing. There is thus no transmigration of souls. Instead, it is believed that the last moment of the dying of one person gives rise to the life of a new-born child who inherits the first person's Karma (Saddhatissa, 19-20). This has been described as similar to the lighting of one candle by another, yet the candles are not the same.

To put this in our own words, it seems to be the Buddhist teaching that the body is like a cloak wrapped around a "soul" (we use quotes because the term is nothing like the soul as generally is understood in Western or Hindu philosophy) which has always existed. The "soul" is like a flow of consciousness which never ceases to exist, or a constant desire for things. This "soul" continues to be purified or defiled depending upon the deeds (Karma) of the person. As one person dies, the state of the "soul" with its deeds comes alive in a new person being born. This goes on until desire has been finally conquered through right thoughts and right action – which are completely one's own efforts, without any outside help except for some human guidance. Buddhists maintain that this is not the same as transmigration of souls. What is passed to another is a person's Karma. Although they still have Reincarnation and Karma, it doesn't seem to have the same sort of "snakes and ladders" quality of Hinduism, where you are constantly being rewarded or punished for what you allegedly did in a former life. It also seems much more hopeful since anyone can do it, and positive since the ethical teachings, if sincerely practiced, would seem to me to make for a better world to live in even without an afterlife.

Appendix 5

A Day of Rest

INTRODUCTION

One of the more remarkable things about the world that we take for granted is the weekly cycle and the common occurrence of a day off in places as diverse as China; Singapore; Fiji; India; Latin America; Scandinavia; Orthodox, Protestant and Catholic Europe; Jewish Israel; Sub-Saharan Africa; the Islamic world stretching from Africa to Indonesia; and in a place as mundane as the United States. In this appendix we will examine the origin of the seven day week and its understanding particularly among Jews, Christians, Muslims and Hindus, with reference to some other groups, most notably the revolutionaries of 18th century France (who briefly established a cult of the goddess "Reason") and the atheists of 20th century Soviet Union.

There is a paucity of material on this subject. It is surprising for a common institution, firmly grounded in common practice around the world (after all, the vast majority of people today have their lives regulated by a seven day week), to have so little scholarly agreement as to its origin, let alone so little relevant literature.

BEFORE THE WEEK

The Calendars that people use and have used are extremely interesting in their variations from one culture to another. In 1982, when I (Douglas) lived in the Middle East, the month of Ramadan (when the faithful of Islam fast from dawn till dusk) fell during the middle of the summer. In 1998 the President of the United States was in a rush to complete a brief bombing "campaign" against Iraq before Ramadan began in December. The month had moved 6 months out of synch with the astronomical year because Islam uses a lunar calendar: the months are the moons – from new to full to new again (Lippman). In the Christian world, the Gregorian calendar (which came into use during the time of Pope

Gregory) is in use and follows an astronomical year, with the months of 28 to 31 days in length being only roughly equivalent to the lunar months, which are about 29 ½ days. In Judaism there is a lunar-solar calendar which roughly maintains the astronomical year by inserting a 13th month, Adar II, every few years. Hinduism has its own calendar, as did many ancient nations. But today, most people on the face of the earth, regardless of which calendar they go by, have a seven day week superimposed over it.

When and where did this cycle of seven start? Moons are easy to observe by people, are regular and, interestingly, have about the same interval as the menstrual period of the human female – perhaps some magic or taboo was seen with each change in women and the lunar orb. But why come up with a shorter, 7 day period that has no astronomical reason? In the Jewish and Christian bible the Sabbath, and thus the 7 day week, is considered to have been given by God at the beginning of humanity (marriage being the only other creation ordinance). The historical evidence, however, is far more difficult to piece together.

In ancient Egypt there were the three ten day "decades" in each of the 30 day civil months. We do not know if there was a day of rest or worship at the conclusion of each decade (Rybczynski, 25). Athenians later had the same sort of 10 day arrangement, although it had nothing to do with holidays, which were specific days each year determined by religious and civic festivities. Rome had 30 or 31 day months with 3 days (for religious activities and the avoidance of some work) dividing them up: Calends (the 1st of the month), Nones (5th or 7th day of the month) and Ides (the 13th or 15th). The Romans later came up with the astronomically correct Julian calendar (perfected in the Gregorian) in 46 BCE, but still had no seven day week.

In China prior to the change to the Gregorian calendar (in 1911) there was a calendar with a 60 day progression of named days. In the Western calendar and week which China adopted, the day off is called Sun Day – the first president of China after the end of the Mongol dynasty was Sun Yat Sen, who was a Christian.

The ancient Maya had a ceremonial 13 day period (Rybczynski, 27).

In Mesopotamia there was commemorated the 14th day of each lunar month, the day of the full moon, called *shabattu* (Bacchiocchi, "Remembering...", 72). It is unclear to me whether this term came to be attached to the Jewish Sabbath, or whether it was in fact an offshoot itself from an older Jewish word derived from the word for seven or week – in other words, whether the day off already existed in another culture and its influence was already beginning to spread. By the seventh century BCE, the 7th, 14th, 21st and 28th days of each Mesopotamian month had become days where certain work was proscribed. This still was not a true week that operated beyond the confines of the monthly cycle, since months could have 29 or 30 days.

Seven had always been an important magical number in the ancient world. It is a prime number and the number of the wandering stars in the night sky (the visible planets of our solar system plus the moon). Seven is, in fact, recognized as a magical number in every part of the world: Babylon, Phoenicia, Greece, Rome, China, India, Africa, the Pacific and the Native American peoples. Astrologically the seven planets came to be associated with seven of the gods, and they in turn became associated with having special influence over certain days and the cycle of seven became common beyond Judaism and Babylon – at least that is the assumption based on the names of the days (Rybczynski, 30-31). There is no specific record or direct evidence of this. Perhaps this cycle of seven was already kept in some way by many of the common people.

In the Roman empire, some evidence exists for a planetary week in the time of Augustus Caesar (1st century CE). At the time of Jesus Christ, there was already a large minority (perhaps as many as 1/7th of the some 60 million people in the Roman Empire were Jewish at the time [Madden; Comay, 115]) that were already keeping a seven day cycle or work and rest/worship. And they had been doing it for at the very least 500 years, and probably much longer. By the time of Dio Cassius (in the 3rd Century CE), the seven day, planetary week was the norm in people's private lives within the Roman Empire.

Jewish Sabbath

Rather than cover material that is taught by Judaism regarding the Sabbath, or go into depth on the Sabbath and Judaism generally, let us briefly consider two aspects of the Jewish understanding and practice.

First is the ability of the day to keep a people distinct (Heschel, 561-2). The keeping of a particular day as something special, a holy time, has served to remind others of a difference between people who keep the Sabbath and their neighbors who do not. This does not always result in positive consequences, people who didn't work one day a week in the early Roman Empire were considered foolish and lazy (Murphy-O'Connor, personal communication), at other times it is seen as a sign of slavish subjection to a way of life that has been superseded. But for those who keep a day off, it serves to strengthen the community, even during times of intense persecution.

Secondly, it is very clear that the Jewish Sabbath observance is the source of the one day in seven day off. Thus the keeping of a 7 day week "rubbed off" on others who came into contact with Jews. The influence of the Jews was the source of a seven day cycle among the Muslims (Durant, *Faith*, 185) and the Romans: The Romans came to associate "Sabbath" with Saturday (the day of Saturn - an unlucky planet since it is the slowest and dimmest of the visible worlds), and with the closing of Jewish businesses on that day. Saturday was the initial planetary day off throughout the Empire. Perhaps for reasons of rising anti-Semitism, especially after the Jewish revolts against Rome (by 135 CE emperor Hadrian outlawed Judaism and particularly Sabbath keeping [Bacchiocchi, *Rest*, 238]), it was later changed for the Romans to Sunday (Ibid., 249 – Tertullian attributes the actual change of rest day [from Saturday to Sunday] in the Roman Empire to Pagans, yet as a Christian he was himself keeping Sunday as a Christian day [Ibid., 312]). This was finalized by Constantine (Rybczynski, 34 40). The somewhat schizophrenic Christian view of the Sabbath will be covered below, but the seven day week (although not necessarily the specific day of rest) used by Christians stems clearly from the Hebrew Bible and the Roman common usage which also was influenced by Judaism, as well as the tremendous importance that the common people in the Roman Empire put on the planetary week by the second century CE (Colson).

CHRISTIANITY – EARLY TO MEDIAEVAL

A survey of current scholarship on the early Christian church shows it to be more of a branch of Judaism than a new religion. It was indistinguishable to outsiders throughout the period in which the "New Testament" was being written. "...early Christians gathered frequently in the agape or love feast, usually on a Sabbath evening," (Durant,

Caesar, 597-598). Could this have been a dinner as a group after Sabbath services – a sort of "church pot luck" at the synagogue? At the very least it would seem to be that the "Christian 'family' [was] following the example of Jewish sabbath [sic] observance," and that there was a "weekly rhythm to the life of the congregation" (Meeks, *First*, 143). No mention is made in the Greek Christian Scriptures or in other records of an abandonment of the Sabbath in the 1st Century CE. This "would have caused tremendous problems within the Jewish and Christian community that would have been recorded" (Carson, quoted by Ford in personal communication). "Jesus' followers observed the Sabbath [sic] rest…:" in the Book of Acts (the earliest history of the new movement after the death of the Founder) Christians were charged with various offences, but "never with breaking the Sabbath" (E.P. Sanders, 221). They may have also been keeping other, annual, "high day" Sabbaths from the Hebrew scriptures (Meeks, *First*, 163), which would lead one to the assumption that the weekly cycle was still maintained in the new group during its first six or seven decades. It is clear that as late as the, "4th and 5th century, we have evidence of Christians still existing within Jewish communities, and we have evidence of members of Christian communities participating in Jewish festivals" (Meeks, "Wrestling").

The excuse that Slaves couldn't keep a Sabbath is not an issue in the historical record. In the early church there is no evidence of agricultural slaves as members of the Christian movement (Meeks, "Paul's"). The early Christian community, like Judaism, was formed of those that were able to attend. The first gentile converts seem to have come from "God fearers:" non-Jews who attended synagogue and kept the moral precepts of the law, without having undergone public baptism (for women) or the pain of circumcision (understandably! – for men). This is a class of people attached to Judaism also known as "proselytes of the gate" (Stern, 257). They were quite numerous in the 1st Century CE, and many were of the upper class in particular, attracted by the high moral standards of Judaism.

As the community had a greater influx of gentiles, particularly those without any previous familiarity with either Judaism or the Hebrew scriptures, coming in and amidst the rising tide of anti-Semitism (as mentioned above), gradually "The Jewish Sabbath was transferred to the Christian Sunday that replaced it in the second century." (Durant, *Caesar*, 599). A weekly cycle remained, except with a new day of rest. It is noteworthy that at this time Christians still remained a minority within the Empire, but the transfer of the day of rest to another day of the week, historically, may have had more to do with the enormous popularity of Mithraism in the second century in the Roman Empire: the sun-worshipping Mithrists celebrated each Sunday [Rybczynski, 36]).

During the next centuries, Sunday became an article of cannon law and remained a rest day. "The church eased the toil of the peasant with Sundays and holydays, on which it was a sin to do 'servile work'" (Durant *Faith*, 559). "Our oxen know when Sunday comes and will not work on that day" (Chateaubriand, iv, 1.4 quoted in ibid.). The day of rest was a time for community, market and worship in Europe.

CHRISTIANITY – MODERN

There are basically three contemporary schools of thought regarding a day of rest and worship during the week. These 3 approaches could be summarized as follows:

1. "New Covenant" Evangelicals – believe in a radical discontinuity between the religion of the Hebrews and Christianity. They often claim that "every day" is a Sabbath to them. No weekly day of rest is discussed in their literature, except in the context of their belief that those who do keep a rest day are somehow in "bondage" or are "Judaizers".
2. Sunday Sabbitarians – Christians that believe the Sabbath has been transferred to Sunday. The Roman Catholic Church's official teaching now seems to fall in this area (John Paul II). They feel that the Resurrection of Christ on Sunday was the act of God that transferred the rest day from Saturday to Sunday.
3. Seventh Day Sabbitarians – Christians and Messianic Jews that keep a Sabbath of some sort, in some manner, on Saturday. These are small and nontraditional branches of Christianity, but the early Christians would have also fallen in this category.

It is interesting to note that the vast majority of general or nominal Christians today follow a non-religious keeping of one or both of the days of the weekend, each week, as rest days. Thus by their actions, most

Christians would have more in common with groups "2" or "3" above than the more austere believers in group "1". The lack of popularity of the obvious logical conclusion of New Covenant Evangelicals speaks volumes: to truly do away with a real day of rest (replacing it with some "spiritual" rest) would lead to results similar to the French Revolution's or the Soviet Union's experience with rest days (see below) – the results would ironically be the same as those of the non-religious.

HINDUISM

The planetary week was adopted by the Hindus some time shortly after 400 CE. As so much else in Hinduism, it came from the outside and was transformed and adopted by the Vendantic religion. Adivara, the first day of the week, became a holiday and market day (Rybczynski, 40). Adivara is the name of the planetary god of the sun, and Sunday is the first day of the week as in Latin and the Germanic languages. Prior to the arrival of the post-Thomasite Christian missionaries in the 1500's, people on the Indian Subcontinent were already keeping one day in seven as a rest day, and it just happened to be both the same day of the week and dedicated to the same planetary god that the Christians kept (much of the early reasoning for a Sunday day of rest given by 2nd Century Christian Theologians seems to have revolved around it being the day of the sun, rather than the day of Christ's resurrection [Bacchiocchi, *Rest*, 250, 312). Quite a coincidence.

ISLAM

The Koran (62:9) requires prayer in the Mosque only on Friday at midday and on 2 annual days. Muslim owned shops are closed before midday on Friday. In Islam, Friday is not a "holyday" as in some Christian or Jewish understanding, yet it is a part of a weekly cycle, and is in the Islamic world a day of rest. Interestingly, Saturday and Sunday are frequently considered by Muslims as unlucky days (Rybczynski, 33). It is definitely a time of community; having seen it ourselves, Houston Smith was right when he wrote, "one of the most impressive sights in the religions of man occurs when, in a dimly lighted mosque, hundreds of men stand shoulder to shoulder, then kneel and prostrate themselves toward Mecca" (323).

Historical research supports the idea that an Islamic day of worship came from Judaism, by which Muhammad was heavily influenced, and was transported to the day before the Sabbath in order to distinguish it in the new faith (Durant, Age of Faith, 185). Friday is not a work holiday necessarily: in Muslim countries public works, newspapers, etc remain open (Lippman).

The Muslim day of prayer, with its roots in Judaism, perhaps was adopted in a way analogous to circumcision in Islam: it was so much a part of the surrounding religious matrix that Muhammad just assumed that it would be done (Anon. *Islam*, 12). The Koran is a short book (only 4/5ths the size of the Greek portion of the Christian Bible), and one without a great deal of detail, so much of Islamic belief and practice grows out of the Hadith (stories about the Prophet) and Islamic judicial rulings and theological studies over the centuries, as well as the surrounding cultural matrix, particularly the Arab culture at the time of the religion's birth. Again we see much of the keeping of a day of rest as something that develops from the private lives of the common people.

This spread (or eruption of a pre-existing popular keeping of some sort of weekly cycle?) of an idea can be seen in the Hindu Week – India is over 2,000 miles East of Mecca and the Jews were just to the North of Mecca – and Muhammad was preaching some 300 years after the Hindus began keeping a seven day cycle.

FRENCH REVOLUTION

In 1793 The French Revolutionaries created a new calendar, one that they claimed was based on reason. The astronomical calendar of 365 days had a new system of months and "weeks" superimposed over it. Months were each 30 days in length, weeks were 10 (naturally, coming from the same nation that brought us the metric system), and there were 5 days for a public festival – 41 days off a year vs. 52 on Sundays alone under the old system. It was designed to dechristianize the French state (Schama, 776), although Sunday and Sabbath keeping was maintained, often clandestinely, by the Catholics and Jews in France during this period.

The contrived system lasted about 13 years. Long weeks without weekends could not have been popular with the common people, and judging by the speed with which it was abandoned and forgotten, it is doubtful that many outside of the fanatical government rulers and their supporters really "bought in" to the system while it was in place.

SOVIET UNION

During the first 20 years of the Soviet Union there were numerous radical social experiments that were carried out by the government. They ran the spectrum from doing away with marriage (a flop) to collectivizing agriculture (a failure that was maintained at great cost of life, productivity and human happiness). One of the ideas that was put into action was the removal of the week. This may have been inspired originally by Voltaire's comment that to do away with religion you must do away with the weekly day of worship (Rybczynski, 45). Staggered shifts within a five day format, which led to chaos, and then a six day week (Herman, 223), which was also never accepted – and always unpopular. The experiment lasted from 1929 until 1940 when the USSR officially returned to the Gregorian Calendar.

OBSERVATIONS FROM MODERN BIOLOGY

One of the unexpected creations of the French Revolution was the total mobilization of a nation's population to wage war. This occurred again during all of the subsequent major wars (Napoleonic Wars, American Civil War, and the two World Wars), as well as during periods of intense social and economic upheaval, such as Stalin's collectivization and industrialization drives. During the First World War, there was a need for ever greater production of war materiel. In the hopes of doing this, the British Government in 1914 began the policy of Sunday work to increase production. Despite more hours and days being worked, less production resulted. When the government reduced hours and returned a Sunday holiday, weekly production increased (Bartley and Chute).

Jeremy Campbell writes of the circaseptan rhythms of the body: heart, blood pressure, temperature, acidity, calcium and cortisol – all of which vary regularly over a period of seven days. Could a day of rest be a natural way of dealing with certain biological fluctuations going on within our bodies? Is the week a pre-wired way of pacing our ordinary lives? Perhaps just as we need to take in food and liquids at certain intervals, and need a certain amount of sleep each night, we also might need a weekly break to prevent fatigue.

CONCLUSION

Religion, "far from being freedom's enemy – can be better understood as a force helping to propel mankind's march toward greater liberty," (Karatnycky). Religion has given us a day off, a day of freedom from other concerns. One wonders how much of the legal rights of working women and men today could be traced back to the institution of a Sabbath (Jewish or Christian), a day of Prayer (Islamic) or holiday (Hindu)? Abraham Lincoln wrote, "As we keep or break the Sabbath day, we nobly save or meanly loose the last and best hope by which man arises" (quoted by Bacchiocchi in "Remember", 69).

What is the relationship between religion and economic structure within cultures? What are the economics of religions or the religious effects on economics? The effect of religion, perhaps driven by a biological (created by God?) need, can very clearly be seen in the adoption of the seven day week. It is one practice that has spread everywhere.

Having a seven-day week and especially a day (or two!) off seems to have struck a cord among people everywhere. Whether it is a biologically programmed need or an ancestral memory or archetype (a taste of Eden?) it is one habit of life that is universal among people. It is the one human institution at the heart of the issue of the relationship between religion and economic creativity and productivity: the day off, the Sabbath, provides a link between individual fundamental needs and corporate duty. On another level, it also provides the time for worship and solidarity with other believers.

Appendix 6

Point of Origin and Philosophy of World Religions

"Three Groups of Three"

1. Religions that originated in *India*:

    Hinduism, Buddhism, and *Jainism*

    *   "Philosophical, introspective, exploring the nature of ultimate reality, pessimistic."

2. Religions that originated in the *Near East*:

    Judaism, Christianity, and *Islam*

    *   "Moralistic, self-assertive, intimate God-man relationship, end-of-the-world belief, man is being saved, optimistic."

3. Religions that originated in the *Orient*:

    Taoism, Confucianism, and *Shintoism*

    *   "Traditional, ancestor worship, the record of the past is a guide for the present, propriety and courage are their ideals. Different from Western concept of worship, no search for ultimate purpose or individual salvation linked to a Divine Being."

(From *What the Great Religions Believe* by Joseph Gaer, p.62.)

Appendix 7

The Golden Rule in Various Traditions

Hinduism – "Do naught to others which, if done to thee, would cause thee pain: this is the sum of duty." *Mahabharata* 5:1517.

Buddhism – "In Five ways should a clansman minister to his friends and familiars...by treating them; as he treats himself." *Sigalovada Sutta* 31.

"Is there a deed, Rahula, thou dost wish to do? Then bethink thee thus: 'Is this deed conductive to my own harm, or to others' harm or to that of both?' Then this is a bad deed, entailing suffering. Such a deed must thou surely not do." *Majjhima Nakaya* 1:415.

Confucianism – "...What you do not want done to yourself, do not do unto others." This "Silver Rule" of Confucius is to be found in three different places in the *Analects*, the sacred scriptures of this religion, but uniformly in the negative form: 5:11; 12:2, 15:23.

Taoism – "To those who are good to me, I am good; and to those who are not good to me, I am also good. And thus all get to be good." " Recompense injury with kindness." *Tao te Ching*.

Zoroastrianism – "That nature only is good when it shall not do unto another whatever is not good for its own self." *Dadistan-I-Dinik*, 94:5.

"Whatever thou dost not approve for thyself, do not approve for any one else. When thou hast acted in this manner, thou art righteous." *Sad Dar* 67:6.

"When a good man is beaten through malice, the effort of every one of you... should continue just as though it happened to himself." *Shayast-na-Shayast* 13:29.

Judaism – "...what thou thyself hatest, do to no man." *Tobit* 4:15.

"Whatsoever thou wouldest that men should not do unto thee, do not do that to them." *Babylonian Talmud*, Shabbath 31a.

Greek Philosophy – "Do not do to others what you would not wish to suffer yourself." (Isocrates).

"Treat your friends as you would want them to treat you." (Diogenes Laertius).

"Do not do what any one is vexed to suffer." (Philo's dictum reported by Eusebius).

Roman Jurisprudence and **Literature** – "Men were brought into existence for the sake of men that they might do one another good." (Cicero).

"What good man regards any misfortune as no concern of his?" (Juvenal).

Christianity – "All things therefore whatsoever ye would that men should do unto you, even so do ye also unto them." Matthew 7:12.

"As ye would that men should do to you, do ye also to them likewise." Luke 6:31.

Only in Christianity is this universal rule of right conduct based upon the character and behavior of God himself: "...I say unto you, love your enemies, and pray for them that persecute you; that ye may be sons of your Father who is in heaven: for he maketh his sun to rise on the evil and the good, and sendeth rain on the just and the unjust." Matthew 5:44-45.

Your Mother – "How would you like it if somebody did that to you?!?"

Appendix 8

Similarities Among the World's Religions

1. *Belief in a Supreme Being*:

Buddhism	Founder
Judaism	Monotheistic
Confucianism	"Supreme Ruler" or "Heaven" (Not actively worshipped.)
Zoroastrianism	Ahura Mazda (good), Angra Mainyu (evil)
Hinduism	Brahma - Worship many deities popularly.
Taoism	Tao
Islam	Allah
Christianity	God

2. *Claim of Divine Incarnation*:

Hinduism	Brahma, Krishna, Rama, Vishnu were all incarnated in men and animals
Buddhism	Buddha
Islam	Shiite Imams are considered incarnations of the prophet.
Christianity	Christ

Claim of a Supernatural Origin of the Founders:

Buddha	Pre-existent heavenly being
Taoism	Lao Tzu born old
Zoroaster	Born of a virgin
Christ	Born of a virgin

3. *Claim of Divine Revelation*:

All claim to possess divinely saving truth, not merely man-made, nor even man-discovered.

4. *Claim of Inspired Scripture*:

   All possess definite sets of documents which are regarded as conveying unique Divine truths which need to be known for salvation.

   The Quran of the Muslims and the Rig Veda of the Hindus are claimed by their people to be verbally inspired and literally infallible.

5. *Report of Miracles Performed*:

   Usually miracles are related in connection with the religion's Founder.

6. *Recognition of a Sacred Community*:

Buddhism	Monks
Christianity	Holy Orders in some denominations
Hinduism	Caste System
Islam	Muslims above infidels

7. *Hope of Universal Religion*:

   Judaism, Zoroastrianism, Buddhism, Islam and Christianity all express their desire of becoming the world's only religion.

8. *Future Life*:

Hinduism and Buddhism	Hope for Nirvana/Moksha
Confucianism	Ghostly future existence.
Zoroastrianism, Christianity and Islam	Heaven and Hell
Taoism	Heavens and Hells
Shintoism	Believe in a continuing life after this, but don't actually concern themselves with it.

Taken from: Hume, Robert E. *The World's Living Religions*. Edinburgh: T. & T. Clark, 1959, pages 270-282.

Appendix 9

Apostles' Creed

1. I believe in God the Father, Almighty, Maker of heaven and earth:

2. And in Jesus Christ, his only begotten Son, our Lord:

3. Who was conceived by the Holy Ghost, born of the Virgin Mary:

4. Suffered under Pontius Pilate; was crucified, dead and buried: He descended into hell:

5. The third day he rose again from the dead:

6. He ascended into heaven, and sits at the right hand of God the Father Almighty:

7. From thence he shall come to judge the quick and the dead:

8. I believe in the Holy Ghost:

9. I believe in the holy catholic church: the communion of saints:

10. The forgiveness of sins:

11. The resurrection of the body:

12. And the life everlasting. Amen.

Appendix 10

Selections from:

Disputation of Doctor Martin Luther on the Power and Efficacy of Indulgences by Dr. Martin Luther (1517)

10. Ignorant and wicked are the doings of those priests who, in the case of the dying, reserve canonical penances for purgatory.

11. This changing of the canonical penalty to the penalty of purgatory is quite evidently one of the tares that were sown while the bishops slept.

12. In former times the canonical penalties were imposed not after, but before absolution, as tests of true contrition.

13. The dying are freed by death from all penalties; they are already dead to canonical rules, and have a right to be released from them.

14. The imperfect health [of soul], that is to say, the imperfect love, of the dying brings with it, of necessity, great fear; and the smaller the love, the greater is the fear.

15. This fear and horror is sufficient of itself alone (to say nothing of other things) to constitute the penalty of purgatory, since it is very near to the horror of despair.

16. Hell, purgatory, and heaven seem to differ as do despair, almost-despair, and the assurance of safety.

17. With souls in purgatory it seems necessary that horror should grow less and love increase.

18. It seems unproved, either by reason or Scripture, that they are outside the state of merit, that is to say, of increasing love.

19. Again, it seems unproved that they, or at least that all of them, are certain or assured of their own blessedness, though we may be quite certain of it.

20. Therefore by "full remission of all penalties" the pope means not actually "of all," but only of those imposed by himself.

21. Therefore those preachers of indulgences are in error, who say that by the pope's indulgences a man is freed from every penalty, and saved;

22. Whereas he remits to souls in purgatory no penalty which, according to the canons, they would have had to pay in this life.

23. If it is at all possible to grant to any one the remission of all penalties whatsoever, it is certain that this remission can be granted only to the most perfect, that is, to the very fewest.

24. It must needs be, therefore, that the greater part of the people are deceived by that indiscriminate and highsounding promise of release from penalty.

25. The power which the pope has, in a general way, over purgatory, is just like the power which any bishop or curate has, in a special way, within his own diocese or parish.

26. The pope does well when he grants remission to souls [in purgatory], not by the power of the keys (which he does not possess), but by way of intercession.

27. They preach man who say that so soon as the penny jingles into the money-box, the soul flies out [of purgatory].

28. It is certain that when the penny jingles into the money-box, gain and avarice can be increased, but the result of the intercession of the Church is in the power of God alone.

Taken from: Published in: *Works of Martin Luther*: Adolph Spaeth, L.D. Reed, Henry Eyster Jacobs, et Al., Trans. & Eds. (Philadelphia: A. J. Holman Company, 1915), Vol.1, pp. 29-38

Appendix 11

Selected Illustrations

A. HINDUISM

Entrance to the Sri Veeramakaliamman Temple,
dedicated to the ferocious goddess Kali.

Close up of an image in the Sri Veeramakaliamman Temple.

Entrance to the Sri Mariamman Temple - the
oldest Hindu temple in Singapore.

B. Buddhism

Gold covered image of the Buddha in the
Siong Lim (Golden Light) Temple.

Entrance Gate to the Buddha in the Siong
Lim Temple in Singapore.

Interior of the Buddhist Lian Shan Shuang Lin Monastery.

C. TAOISM AND CONFUCIANISM

Painting representing Lao Tzu the founder of Taoism.

Woodcut representing Kung Fu-tse (Confucius)
the founder of Confucianism.

D. Islam

Painting representing Mohammed the prophet of Islam.

A Mosque in the heart of a modern city in south Asia.

E. CHRISTIANITY

A gold covered statue of the Virgin Mary from the roof of the Papal Palace at Avignon, France. From 1309 to 1378 seven Popes resided in Avignon rather than in Rome.

Painting of Martin Luther founder of the Lutheran church.

Illustration of John Calvin founder of the Reform movement, of which the Presbyterian church is the largest fellowship.

Illustration of John Wesley founder of the Methodist church.

Woodcut representing a Quaker Assembly taking place.

A photograph taken in 1843 of Joseph Smith
founder of the Church Of Jesus Christ Of The
Latter Day Saints (Mormon chruch).

A photograph of Mary Baker Eddy founder of the Church
Of Christ Scientist (Christian Science church).

A photograph of William Booth late in life. General
Booth was the founder of the Salvation Army.

A photograph of Charles Taze Russell (1852-1916)
the original Founder of the Jehovah's Witnesses.

A photograph of "Judge" Joseph Rutherford who succeeded
Charles Taze Russell as the leader of the Jehovah's
Witnesses upon the latter's death in 1916. Judge Rutherford
greatly altered the Church's initial teachings.

Charles Parham, a Methodist minister in Topeka, Kansas, came to believe that Glossolalia, speaking in tongues, was the only evidence of a "second baptism". During a revival meeting on January 1, 1901, Agnes Ozman, one of his pupils, became the first person to "speak in tongues." By the first decade of the twenty-first century it was estimated that almost 10% of the world's population attend Pentecostal churches or are charismatic members of major church denominations.

Appendix 12

World Religions Glossary

AHIMSA: To Jains non-violence; not to injure any living thing.

AHURA MAZDA: Supreme Deity of the Zoroastrians; means the Lord of Light or Wise Lord.

ALCHEMY: Miraculous changes from one form to another.

ALLAH: One true God of the Muslims. Also used as the word for God by Christian Arabs.

AMATERASU: Shinto sun goddess; chief among god and goddesses.

AMITABHA: One of the Buddhas particularly honored among the Oriental Buddhists.

ANGRA MAINYU: Also known to Zoroastrians as Ahriman. The spirit of evil in opposition to Ahura Mazda.

ANIMISM: The belief that everything in nature has a spirit or soul.

ANTHROPOMORPHISM: Attributing human characteristics to God or gods.

ATHEISM: Denial of any supernatural power or deity.

ATMAN: In Hinduism it represents the Universal Self.

AVESTA: Sacred Scriptures of Zoroastrians.

BAR MIZVAH: In Judaism at thirteen, it is a ceremony marking his entrance to manhood.

BHAGAVAD GITA: An epic poem. Most loved religious writing of Hinduism.

BHAKTI: Religious devotion in the Hindu faith.

BODHISATTVA: A Buddha to be or a candidate for becoming a Buddha.

BRAHMA: Hindu creator god; a member of the three-in-one Trimurti.

BRAHMAN: The Hindu term for the "World Soul"

BRAHMIN: Top caste of Hinduism--are priests and holy men.

BUDDHA: The "Awakened" or "Enlightened" One. Siddhartha Gautama. Also, can mean what others may become.

CALIPH: A political, religious leader and successor of Muhammad.

CHUN-TZU: The ideal man to the Confucians.

DHARMA: The law of the universe. In Buddhism, it is Buddha's doctrine.

GURU: A Hindu spiritual teacher.

HAJJ: Arabic word for the pilgrimage to be made to Mecca by Muslims.

HINAYANA: Means the "lesser vehicle." The same as Theravada Buddhism.

HSIAO: In Confucianism, it means filial piety.

I CHING: Classic Handbook of divination of the Confucians.

IMAM: Divinely appointed successor of the Shiites to Muhammad. Similar to a Caliph of the Sunni branch.

JEN: Concern for humanity; a quality for Confucians to seek.

JIHAD: Muslim holy war.

KA'BA: Cube-shaped shrine in Mecca. A sacred symbol of Islam.

KAMI: Word for Shinto gods.

KARMA: Law of cause and effect.

KOJIKI: Shinto sacred writings.

KRISHNA: An Avatar of Vishnu. Well-loved hero in Hinduism.

KSHATRIYA: Second rank of Hindu caste.

LI: Propriety: good form. Major quality of Confucius.

MAHAYANA: "Great Raft" larger, more liberal form of Buddhism.

MANTRA: Sacred word or saying usually used in meditation.

MESSIAH: In Judaism, the Anointed One who is to come to set up the Kingdom of God. The Greek word for Anointed One is "Christ."

MOKSHA: Means emancipation to Hindus and Buddhists. Salvation from physical life/the cycle of death and rebirth. Ultimate goal of man.

MYTH: The sacred writings of a religion which give direction and meaning to life.

NIRVANA: Cessation of craving or desire; release. The ultimate goal of Buddhists.

QUR'AN (KORAN): Divine revelation of Allah to Muhammad, written in Arabic. Holy book of Muslims.

SHAMAN: Holy man who sometimes uses magic.

SHI'A: The second largest Muslim branch. Name means "the party which follows Ali" (Ali was the fourth caliph after Muhammad, and also his cousin and father-in-law).

SHIVA: The Destroyer and one of the Trimurti of Hinduism.

SIKH: A disciple of Nanak--follower of Sikhism.

SUDRAS: Lowest caste of Hinduism--commoners.

SUNNI: The major Muslim branch. It is considered to have the orthodox beliefs.

SUTRA: Written teachings of Buddha or a saint; looked upon as sacred writing.

TABOO: Prohibition of the use of sacred objects.

TALMUD: Jewish commentary on the Torah.

TANTRISM: Hindu religious movement which delves into mysticism and magic.

TAO TE CHING: Lao Tzu's writing which is used for Taoist scripture.

TAO: To Confucians and Taoists it means the cosmic way. It is more reverenced by the Taoists.

THERAVADA: Means "Way of the Elders." The more conservative branch of Buddhism. Synonymous with Hinayana.

TORAH: The Law; Most specifically the first five books of the Holy Scriptures of Judaism.

VAISHYA: Third in rank of the Hindu caste system.

VEDA: Means "knowledge." The oldest Hindu writings.

VISHNU: The Preserver and one of the three deities of the Trimurti of the Hindus.

WU WEI: The heart and core of Taoist philosophy. Means non-action.

YANG: One of the two energy forces--the masculine, bright, positive side in Taoism and Confucianism.

YIN: The second of the two energy forces--the feminine, dark, and negative side in Taoism and Confucianism.

YOGA: Inner discipline leading to the way of salvation.

ZEN: The belief that enlightenment can be attained through meditation rather than teachings. A form of Buddhism.

Appendix 13

Christian Denominations Glossary

AGNOSTICISM: The belief that the reality of God cannot be known. From the Greek, the literal meaning is "no-knowledge."

ANATHEMA: A thing devoted to evil, or a curse.

ANTHROPOMORPHISM: Ascribing to God human qualities, i.e., God is described as "walking in the garden in the cool of the day" (Gen. 3:8).

ARIANISM: T he belief that Jesus has not always existed (created by the Father) and that Jesus is a separate and distinct entity from the Father.

ATHEISM: The denial of the existence of a personal, moral, supreme being.

CATECHISM: A systematic study of religion usually in question and answer form.

CHARISMATIC: Literally means, "possessing free gifts"--refers to the gifts of I Corinthians 12:8-10 (faith, healing miracles, prophecy, tongues--with emphasis on tongues-speaking).

CONSUBSTANTIATION: The belief that the bread and wine do not actually become the body and blood of Christ, but Christ somehow lives in these elements during the communion service.

CONTRITION: Sorrow for sins.

DOCETISM: A term generally used for those who emphasize the Divinity of Christ over His humanity.

DOGMA: Church teaching set forth beyond dispute.

ECUMENICAL: representing a wide body of churches.

EPIPHANY: Literally the appearance of God. The Catholic feast celebrated January 6 celebrating the appearance of God in human form, Jesus.

ESCHATOLOGY: Having to do with the end time; i.e., the study of Old Testament Eschatology is the study of Old Testament end time prophecy; the doctrine of last things, end of the age.

EUCHARIST: Literally "thanksgiving," from the Greek. Refers to communion service during mass, the partaking of bread wafers.

EVANGELICAL: Refers to churches or organizations that emphasize preaching a message (from Greek, "evangelion"--"good tidings").

FUNDAMENTALISM: The emphasis of the literal interpretation of the HOLY BIBLE and basic Protestant doctrine.

GNOSTICISM: The belief that salvation is accomplished by deliverance of the spirit from its captivity in the world through secret knowledge.

IMMACULATE CONCEPTION: The idea that Mary was conceived without original sin.

INDULGENCE: The remission granted by the church of the temporal punishment due to sins already forbidden.

LITANY: The part of the liturgy in which the officiating clergyman reads a line and the congregation responds.

LITURGY: Consists of the acts of worship or ceremony that occur in the church; is the name for the Eastern Orthodox Service.

PENANCE: The sacrament by which sins committed after baptism are forgiven through the absolution of the Priest.

SYNCRETISM: A word derived from the Greek "syncretizein"--"to hold together like Cretans"; it denotes any form of religion in which elements from more than one original religious tradition are combined.

TRANSUBSTANTIATION: The belief that the bread and wine in the communion services actually become the body and blood of Christ.

BIBLIOGRAPHY

Adler, Mortimer J. *How to Think About God.* NY, NY: MacMillan, 1980.

Adler, Mortimer J. *Ten Philosophical Mistakes.* NY, NY: MacMillan, 1985.

Adler, Mortimer J. *The Angels and Us.* NY, NY: MacMillan, 1982.

Ahrens, John. "Nature and Human Values." *www.hanover.edu/philos/john/mss/hcpubfnl.html.* February 25, 1999.

Alalibo, Allswell. Personal communication.

Anon. *Christianity.* New York: LIFE Educational Reprints, n.d.

Anon. *The Faiths of China.* New York: LIFE Educational Reprints, n.d.

Anon. *Hinduism.* New York: LIFE Educational Reprints, n.d.

Anon. *The Law of Judaism.* New York: LIFE Educational Reprints, n.d.

Anon. "Moral Concepts And Theories." *http://ethics.tamu.edu/ethics/essays/moral.htm.* February 25, 1999.

Anon. *The Path of Buddhism.* New York: LIFE Educational Reprints, n.d.

Anon. "What Scientology Teaches." *Christianity Today* (September 17,1982), p.33.

Anon. *The World of Islam.* New York: LIFE Educational Reprints, n.d.

Anon. "You Can Live Forever in Paradise on Earth". Brooklyn, New York: Watchtower Bible and Tract Society of New York, Inc., 1982.

Apostolic Fathers. *Early Christian Writings.* Maxwell Staniforth, Trans. NY: Dorset, 1986.

Arberry, A. *The Koran Interpreted.* New York: MacMillan, 1955.

Armstrong, Karen. *A History of God.* NY: Knopf, 1993.

Asheri, Mordechai. *Living Jewish.* New York: Everest House, 1978.

Augsburger, David W. *Pastoral Counseling Across Cultures.* Philadelphia: Westminster, 1986.

Bacchiocchi, Samuele. "Remembering the Sabbath" *The Sabbath in Jewish and Christian Traditions.* New York: Cross Road, 1991.

Bacchiocchi, Samuele. *Divine Rest for Human Restlessness.* Berrien Springs, Mich.: Biblical Perspectives, 1988.

Backman, Milton. *Christian Churches of America Origins and Beliefs.* Utah: Brigham Young Press, 1976.

Barraclough, Geoffrey. *The Times Atlas of World History.* London: Times Books, 1997.

Bartley, S.Howard and Eloise Chute. *Fatigue and Impairment in Man.* New York: McGraw-Hill, 1947.

Bergant, Dianne. *Job, Ecclesiasties.* Wilmington, DE: Michael Glazer, 1982.

Book of Mormon. Salt Lake City: Church of Jesus Christ of Latter-day Saints, 1981.

Bourke, Vernon J., ed. *The Pocket Aquinas.* NY, NY: Washington Square Press, 1960.

Bronowski, Jacob. "Black Magic and White Magic." *The World Treasury of Physics, Astronomy, and Mathematics.* Boston, MA: Little, Brown and Company, 1991.

Burr, John R. and Milton Goldinger. *Philosophy and Contemporary Issues.* Upper Saddle River, NJ: Prentice Hall, 1996.

Burrows, Millar. *Founders of Great Religions.* New York: Books for Libraries Press, 1973.

Burton, Richard Francis. *Pilgrimage to Medina and Mecca.* Frederick, MD: Recorded Books, 1992 (Sound Recording).

Bush, Richard C. *Religion in China.* Niles, Illinois: Argus Communication, 1977.

Callinicos, Rev. Constantine N. *The Greek Orthodox Catechism.* New York: Greek Archdiocese of North and South America, 1960.

Campbell, Jeremy. *Winston Churchill's Afternoon Nap: A Wide-Awake Inquiry Into the Human Nature of Time.* New York: Knopf, 1986.

Camus, Albert. "The Unbeliever." *The World Treasury of Modern Religious Thought.* Boston, MA: Little, Brown and Company, 1990.

Champion, Selwyn G. *The Eleven Religions and Their Proverbial Lore.* New York: E. P. Dutton & Co., Inc., 1973.

Chateaubriand, Vicomte de. *The Genius of Christianity.* Baltimore: n.p., n.d.

Cohen, Daniel. *The New Believers.* New York: M. Evans & Co., Inc., 1975.

Colson, D.A., Ed. *From Sabbath to the Lord's Day.* Grand Rapids, Mich.: Zondervan, 1982.

Colson, F.H. *The Week.* Cambridge: 1926.

Comay, Joan. *The Diaspora Story*. New York: Random House, 1980.

Cortesi, David E. "Looking for an Ethical Touchstone." *www.dsp.net/cortesi/unbelieving/ethical*. March 1, 1999.

Crabb, Larry. *Understanding People*. Grand Rapids, Michigan: Zondervan, 1987.

de Liguorgi, St. Aiphonsus. *The Glories of Mary*. Baltimore, Maryland: Helicon Press, 1963.

Durant, Will *The Age of Faith*. New York: Simon and Schuster, 1950.

Durant, Will. *Caesar and Christ*. New York: Simon and Schuster, 1944.

Eaton, Albert William. *The Faith, History and Practice of the Church of England*. London, England: Hodder and Stoughton, 1959.

Edgerton, Franklin, (Translator). *Bhagavad-Gita*. Massachusetts: Harvard University Publishing, 1981.

Ellwood, Robert S. *Many Peoples, Many Faiths*. Englewood Cliffs, New Jersey: Prentice-Hall, 1976.

Erickson, Millard J. *Introducing Christian Doctrine*. Grand Rapids, MI: Baker, 1992.

Eusebius. *Church History*. G.A. Williamson, Trans. NY: Dorset, 1984.

Favier, Jean. *Gold and Spices*. New York: Holmes and Meier, 1998.

Ford, Desmond. *The Forgotten Day*. Newcastle, Calif.: Desmond Ford Publications, 1981.

Fox, Robin Lane. *Pagans and Christians*. NY: Knopf, 1989.

Freud, Sigmund. "The Future of an Illusion." *The World Treasury of Modern Religious Thought*. Boston, MA: Little, Brown and Company, 1990.

Fromkin, David. "How the Modern Middle East Map Came to be Drawn." *Smithsonian*, May, 1991.

Frost, S.E. *Basic Teachings of the Great Philosophers*. Garden City, NY: Dolphin Books, 1962.

Gabriel, Mark. *Jesus and Muhammad*. Lake Mary, FL: Front Line, 2004.

Gaer, Joseph. *What the Great Religions Believe*. New York: Signet, 1963.

Gensler, Harry J. "The Golden Rule." *www.jcu.edu/philosophy/gensler/goldenrule.htm*. February 25, 1999.

Gensler, Harry J. *Formal Ethics*. Routledge, 1996.

Gert, Bernard. "Morality versus Slogans." *http://aristotle.tamu. edu~rasmith/Courses/251/gert-paper.html*. February 25, 1999.

Gibb, Hamilton. "The Foundations of Islamic Thought." *The World Treasury of Modern Religious Thought*. Boston, MA: Little, Brown and Company, 1990.

Gibbon, Edward. "The Progress of the Christian Religion." *The World Treasury of Modern Religious Thought*. Boston, MA: Little, Brown and Company, 1990.

Grabbe, Lester. *First Century Judaism*. Edinburgh, Scotland: T&T Clark, 1996.

Grant, Michael. *The Fall of the Roman Empire*. NY: Collier, 1990.

Green, Jay E. *100 Great Thinkers*. New York: Pocket Books, 1967.

Hayward, Alan. *Great News for the World*. Aylesbury, England: Hazell Watson Viney, Ltd., 1976.

Heisenberg, Werner. "Positivism, Metaphysics, and Religion." *The World Treasury of Physics, Astronomy, and Mathematics*. Boston, MA: Little, Brown and Company, 1991.

Herman, Victor. *Coming Out of the Ice*. New York: Harcourt Brace Jovanovich, 1979.

Herschel, Abraham. "The Spirit of Judaism" *The World Treasury of Modern Religious Thought*. Boston, MA: Little, Brown and Company, 1990.

Hick, John. "The Problem of Evil," *Philosophy and Contemporary Issues*. Upper Saddle River, NJ: Prentice Hall, 1996.

Holt, Jim. "Quizzing the Philosophers". *Wall Street Journal*, 21 August 1998.

Holy Bible – New King James Version. Nashville, Tennessee: Nelson Publishers, 1982.

Holy Scriptures. Philadelphia: Jewish Publication Society, 1917.

Hopfe, Lewis M. *Religions of the World*. New York: Macmillan, 1983.

Hourani, A. *History of the Arab Peoples*. New York: Werner Books, 1991.

Hubbard, L. Ron. *Dianetics*. Los Angeles, California: Bridge Publications, 1982.

Hume, Robert E. *The World's Living Religions*. Edinburgh: T. & T. Clark, 1959.

Hutchison, John. A. *Paths of Faith*. New York: McGraw-Hill, 1975.

Ibn Khaldun. *The Muqaddimah*. Princeton: Princeton University, 1969.

Iqbal, Muhammad. "The Reconstruction of Tradition." *The World Treasury of Modern Religious Thought*. Boston, MA: Little, Brown and Company, 1990.

Jackson, Samuel Macauley (Editor-in-chief). *The New Schaff-Herzog Encyclopedia of Religious Knowledge*. McMillan: Baker Book House, 1989.

Jenkins, Philip. *The Next Christianity*. New York: Oxford University Press, 2002.

Johnson, B.C. "God and the Problem of Evil," *Philosophy and Contemporary Issues*. Upper Saddle River, NJ: Prentice Hall, 1996.

Jones, Judy and William Wilson. *An Incomplete Education*. New York: Ballantine Books, 1987.

Karatnycky, Adrian. "Freedom and Faith." *Wall Street Journal*, 22 January, 1999.

Kitagawa, Joseph M. "Buddhism in the Modern World." *The World Treasury of Modern Religious Thought*. Boston, MA: Little, Brown and Company, 1990.

Koran. N. J. Dawood (Translator). London: Penguin Books, 2000.

Kushner, Harold S. *When Bad Things Happen to Good People*. NY, NY: Avon, 1982.

Kuykendall, Kenneth L. "East Asian Religions." Online. California State University. *http://www.csudh.edu/hux/syllabi/547/default.htm*. Accessed 23 May 2000.

Lao Tzu. Victor H. Mair (translator) *Tao Te Ching*. New York: Quality Paperback Book Club, 1998.

Lewis, Bernard. *The Crisis of Islam*. New York: Modern Library, 2003.

Lewis, Bernard. *What Went Wrong?* New York: Oxford University Press, 2002.

Lewis, Clive Staples. *The Abolition of Man*. New York, NY. Touchstone, 1996.

Lippman, Thomas W. *Understanding Islam*. Ashland, Oregon: Blackstone, 1991 (Sound Recording).

Luther, Martin. *Works of Martin Luther*. Adolph Spaeth, L.D. Reed, Henry Eyster Jacobs, et Al., Trans. & Eds. Philadelphia: A. J. Holman Company, 1915.

MacIver, Robert M. "The Deep Beauty of the Golden Rule." *Philosophy and Contemporary Issues*. Upper Saddle River, NJ: Prentice Hall, 1996.

Madden, John. "Slavery in the Roman Empire: Numbers and Origins." Classics Ireland, 1996 Volume 3. *http://www.ucd.ie/~classics*, accessed 20 Oct 1998.

Maimonides, Moses: *Guide to the Perplexed*. M. Friedländer (translator). Online. http://www.sacred-texts.com/jud/gfp/index.htm. Accessed 23 May 2004.

Marx, Karl. "Religion, the Opiate of the People." *The World Treasury of Modern Religious Thought*. Boston, MA: Little, Brown and Company, 1990.

Matt, Daniel C. *The Essential Kabbalah*. New York: Quality Paperback Book Club, 1998.

McBrien, Richard P. *Catholicism*. Minneapolis, Minnesota: Winston Press, 1981.

McDowell, Josh, and Don Stewart. *Handbook of Today's Religions*. San Bernardino, California: Here's Life Publishing, 1983.

Mead, Frank S. *Handbook of Denominations*. Nashville, Tennessee: Abingdon Press, 1980.

Meeks, Wayne. "Paul's Congregations." *http://www.pbs.org/wgbh/pages/fromjesustochrist*, accessed 10/20/1998.

Meeks, Wayne. "Wrestling With Their Jewish Heritage." *http://www.pbs.org/wgbh/pages/fromjesustochrist*, accessed 10/20/1998.

Meeks, Wayne. *The First Urban Christians*. New Haven, Conn.: Yale University, 1983.

Meeks, Wayne. *The Origins of Christian Morality*. New Haven, Conn.: Yale University, 1995.

Mellert, Robert B. "The Future of God." *The Futurist*, Oct. 1999

Miller, Barbara Stoler, (Translator). *Bhagavad-Gita*. New York: Quality Paperback Book Club, 1998.

Mitchell, Robert Cameron. *African Primal Religions*. Niles, Illinois: Argus Communications, 1977.

Morrow, Louis L. *My Catholic Faith*. Wisconsin: My Mission House, 1966.

Murphy-O'Connor, Jerome. *Paul: A Critical Life*. Oxford, UK: Clarendon, 1996.

Murphy-O'Connor, Jerome. Personal communication, June 22, 1995.

Murray, Gilbert. "Failure of Nerve." *The World Treasury of Modern Religious Thought*. Boston, MA: Little, Brown and Company, 1990.

Nagel, Thomas. *What Does it all Mean?* New York, NY: Oxford University Press, 1987.

Nasr, Seyyed Hossein. "The Prophet and Prophetic Religion." *The World Treasury of Modern Religious Thought.* Boston, MA: Little, Brown and Company, 1990.

Nietzsche, Friedrich. "Beyond Good and Evil." *The World Treasury of Modern Religious Thought.* Boston, MA: Little, Brown and Company, 1990.

Noss, David & John. *Man's Religions.* New York: MacMillan, 1984.

Noss, John B. *History of the World's Religions.* New York: Macmillan, 1992.

Oxford Family Encyclopedia. "Buddhism." London: George Philip, 1997.

Oxford Family Encyclopedia. "Hinduism." London: George Philip, 1997.

Peters, Ted. *God as Trinity.* Louisville, KY: Westminster/John Knox, 1993.

Pew Forum on Religion and Public Life. "Pentecostalism". *http://pewforum.org/docs/?DocID=140.* Accessed 11 November 2008.

Polk, W. *The Arab World Today.* Cambridge, MA: Harvard University, 1991.

Pope John Paul II. *Dies Domini.* Pastoral letter, 31 May 1998.

Primus, John H. "Sunday: The Lord's Day as a Sabbath." *The Sabbath in Jewish and Christian Traditions.* New York: Cross Road, 1991.

Pritchard, John. "Worldmapper Datasets 551-582: Religion." SASI, University of Sheffield, *http://www.sheffield.ac.uk/sasi.* Accessed March 26, 2008.

Radhakrishnan, Sarvepalli. "Mysticism and Ethics in Hindu Thought." *The World Treasury of Modern Religious Thought.* Boston, MA: Little, Brown and Company, 1990.

Rahman, Fazlur. "The Qur'an." *The World Treasury of Modern Religious Thought.* Boston, MA: Little, Brown and Company, 1990.

Reader's Digest Almanac & Yearbook 1982. Pleasantville, New York: Reader's Digest, 1982.

Roberts, D. S. *Islam: A Concise Introduction.* San Francisco: Harper and Row, 1981.

Rosten, Leo. *Religions in America.* New York: Simon and Schuster, 1975.

Rowley, Peter. *New Gods in America*. New York: David McKay Co., Inc., 1971.

Rybczynski, Witold. *Waiting For The Weekend*. New York: Viking, 1991.

Saddhatissa, Hammalawa. *An Introduction to Buddhism.* London: Buddhist Vihara, n.d.

Sanders, J. Oswald, and J. Stafford Wright. *Some Modern Religions*. London, England: Inter-Varsity Press, 1969.

Sanders, J. Oswald. *Heresies and Cults*. London, England: Lowe and Brydone Printers, 1969.

Sanders, E.P. *The Historical Figure of Jesus*. London: Allen Lane, 1993.

Sargant, William. *Battle for the Mind*. London: William Heinemann, 1957.

Schama, Simon. *Citizens*. New York: Knopf, 1989.

Smith, Huston. *The Religions of Man*. New York: HarperPerennial, 1986.

Solomon, Victor. *A Handbook on Conversions to the Religions of the World*. Connecticut: Stravon Publishers, 1965.

Soon, Gibson Guo Sen (compiler), Zhang Lent (translator). *Filial Piety Sutra*. Singapore: Internal Printers, n.d.

Stern, David H. *Jewish New Testament Commentary*. Clarksville, Maryland: JNTP, 1996.

Tagore, Ravindranath. "The Four Stages of Life." *The World Treasury of Modern Religious Thought*. Boston, MA: Little, Brown and Company, 1990.

Talmage, James E. *The Articles of Faith.* Salt Lake City, Utah: The Church of Jesus Christ of the Latter Day Saints, 1982.

Teoh, K.J., Teoh Hai Siang (translators). *Cause and Effect*. Singapore: Internal Printers, n.d.

Thurman, Robert A. F., (translator). *The Tibetan Book of the Dead*. New York: Quality Paperback Book Club, 1998.

Trustees of the British Museum. *British Museum Guide*. London: British Museum, 1978.

Various. *Abingdon Dictionary of Living Religions*. Nashville, Tennessee: Abingdon Press, 1981.

Various. *Eerdman's Handbook to Christianity in America*. Grand Rapids, Michigan: William B. Eerdman's Publishing Co., 1983.

Various *Eerdman's Handbook to the World's Religions*. Grand Rapids, Michigan: William B. Eerdmans Publishing, 1982.

Von Huegel, Friedrich. "The Three Elements of Religion." *The World Treasury of Modern Religious Thought*. Boston, MA: Little, Brown and Company, 1990.

Waley, Arthur (Translator). *The Analects of Confucius*. New York: Vintage Books, 1938.

Webster, Hutton. *Rest Days*. New York: Macmillan, 1916 (reprinted by Omnigraphics in 1992).

Westminster Confession of Faith. London, England: Wickliffe Press, 1958.

White, Ellen G. *The Great Controversy*. California: Pacific Press, 1976.

World Almanac & Book of Facts 1984. New York: Newspaper Enterprise, 1983.

World Christian Database. Online: http://www.worldchristiandatabase. org/wcd/. Accessed December 10, 2008.

ABOUT THE AUTHORS

Gary E. Antion, MA

Gary E. Antion holds a Master's Degree in Marriage, Family and Child Therapy from California Family Study Center in North Hollywood (Now called Phillips Institute). In addition, he completed eighteen graduate hours of theology from Southern Methodist University and has taught Comparative Religion courses at the college level for over 25 years. Having served in the ministry in England, Canada and various cities in the United States, he has also served as College Administrator and Associate Professor of Theology.

His travels have taken him to Europe, Australia, the Middle East and the Far East, allowing him to work personally with individuals who were members of various faiths and gain insights into their religious backgrounds. All of his experiences have added to his knowledge of the religions of this world.

Mr. Antion has lectured in several cities worldwide and brought his knowledge of world religion to thousands.

Douglas Ruml, CFM, MA

Doug's Masters degree was completed at the California State University. He has lived in or extensively visited countries in North America, Latin America, Western Europe, Eastern Europe, the Middle East, East Asia, South Asia, Australia, the Caribbean, Melanesia and Polynesia.

Doug is an entrepreneur and also an Adjunct Professor in Graduate Schools at Ohio Dominican University, Ashland University and Franklin University. His work on this book springs from his interest in human cultures, and the tremendous effect religion has had on the various civilizations of humanity right up until the present day.